creative gardening
for busy people

Graham A. Pavey

André Deutsch

First published in 1999 by
André Deutsch Limited
76 Dean Street
London W1V 5HA
www.vci.co.uk

A catalogue record for this book is available
from the British Library

ISBN 0 233 99452 1

Designed by Focus Publishing, Sevenoaks,
Kent (Tel: 01732 742456)

Printed and bound in Great Britain by
Butler & Tanner Ltd, Frome and London

creative gardening for busy people

contents

Introduction

As a professional garden designer most of the gardens I work on are for garden owners who are not gardeners, do not want to be gardeners, but like gardens and enjoy being in and looking at them. They appreciate the need to work in the garden, but regard that work as a chore and not a pleasure. Over the years, I have developed ways of reducing costs and keeping maintenance to a minimum while at the same time making sure that design and construction remain at a high standard. In this book I want to explore the pitfalls of creating and running a garden and then look at some possible solutions, so that the busy garden owner can approach the garden with more confidence and less fear.

The term 'outside room' is frequently used by garden designers these days. It is true that the garden is, and should be, part of the home, but it generally requires more work and can be a daunting and worrying place for some people. Techno-fear, or a fear of modern technology, is a new phenomenon, but horto-fear has been with us for many years and is far more widespread. In this book I intend to lay open many of the myths and legends associated with gardening and equip the layman with the knowledge he needs to create and maintain a garden without becoming a slave to it.

In the past, middle- to upper-class homes would have employed at least one gardener. In Victorian Britain some gardeners enjoyed celebrity status, tempted from garden to garden by ever more generous patrons. As times changed and the large garden retinues began to shrink, many of these expert gardeners turned to writing books and contributing to magazines and, much later, became the original presenters on radio and television shows. They brought with them years of practical experience, and you knew that the advice they gave came from knowledge gained at first hand. As these experts have retired they have gradually been replaced not by practical gardeners, but by nurserymen and younger people who better fit the requirements of the modern media. Modern gardening techniques still rely very heavily on writings from the past, with few opportunities for gaining experience in small private gardens. This means that gardening tips are often recycled, sometimes distorted over time, whether or not they work, resulting in some areas of gardening remaining stagnant and not moving with the times. In many ways we have not escaped the Victorians.

Gardening has to move on – not least because few people nowadays can afford the luxury of a gardener and have to do the work themselves. Busier lives dictate not only that the garden must look after itself more, but also that it must become a place of relaxation – a bolt-hole from the pressures that life throws at all of us.

✿ Anticipation and mystery have been created by this gateway in a garden designed by Lady Tollemarche.

Chapter 1

Educating Gardeners

The education of a garden designer

Before making garden design my life I worked in computers: for eighteen years I had a 'good' job, but I found it tedious and uninspiring work. To combat this assault on my senses, I spent much of my spare time in the garden.

Frankly, I was less of a gardener, more a plant collector. Every weekend would be spent scouring local garden centres and nurseries for additions to my collection. There was little thought put into anything that I did and I made a lot of mistakes. Often I would buy a plant, plant it, nurture it, watch it die or outgrow its patch, dig it up and then replace it. Occasionally the process would be repeated. But I was learning. I learnt that not all the advice given to me was terribly reliable: I was once sold a dwarf larch for my rockery and over the following year or so watched it grow, and grow, and grow; I worried when the needles fell off in the winter and then marvelled when they reappeared the following spring. And it continued to grow and grow. The fact is that no such thing as a dwarf larch exists – they are all extremely large forest trees!

The good thing about the garden and gardening is that it does not bite back. You can be in total control in your own little world, where problems are of no importance – dig it up and start again! As an antidote to a stressful life there are few equals.

During my long train journeys to work, I would nearly always have my head stuck in a gardening book or magazine. I learnt my first long Latin name – *Asplenium scolopendrium*

'Cristatum' – which I had to repeat to myself over and over again for a week until it stuck in my head; it is curious how my brain is now full of such names and remembers new ones easily, but finds it difficult to remember my latest PIN number!

Many of my mistakes are still being made the length and breadth of the country. But I was beginning to understand the problems, as well as the basics of gardening, and that knowledge has been invaluable down the years. It has helped me to understand a client's thinking and better interpret his or her requirements, and aspirations, when discussing a new garden.

Eventually computers overwhelmed me, and I was determined to change my life. But what else could I do? It had to be something connected with gardens, and I had heard about people who made a living designing them for other people. I had no idea what garden design was, but it sounded right for me. So I enrolled on a garden design course at the Chelsea Physic Garden in London.

I remember thinking, before the course began, that my knowledge of plants and gardening was extensive and all I needed to learn was presentation and drawing skills. Ha! I had no idea that a subject could be so large, and so diverse. My knowledge at the time was merely a scratch on the surface.

During the course we met and were taught by many leading, and highly gifted, designers and horticultural professionals. This was useful in enabling me to develop my own style, but it also showed me an aspect which I was only later to realize was far from being true to life. Being at the top of their profession, these designers did not have to worry about such mundane things as the size of a client's purse or how much time it might take to maintain the new garden. The course was invaluable, and I find it hard to imagine how anyone could progress as a designer without such a solid grounding, but it did send me out into the world with rose-tinted spectacles.

Once I began to ply my trade as a working designer, it quickly became apparent that budgets were often quite tiny and there was frequently very little manpower available to maintain the new garden. The best design cannot always be achieved, and each one involves a lot of compromises. The aspirations of the client, the budget and the constraints of the site all contribute, in varying degrees, to chipping away at the potential award-winning design. A successful garden is one created through a partnership between the designer, the contractor (better known as the landscape gardener), the suppliers (mainly nurserymen) and the client. If any of these fail, so can the project. And always, the buck stops with the designer. What started out as one of the best jobs in the world was quickly beginning to lose its shine.

There seemed to be problems at every stage. The only answer was to buckle down and devise ways around them – solutions which would enable me to please the clients, oversee the contractors and nurserymen, and achieve my aim of creating well-designed gardens.

Landscaping

I was very fortunate in my early days to become involved with a local landscape gardener who shares my desire to produce work of the highest standard. We still work together on many projects. Even then, there were areas of construction which concerned me. These were problems associated not with standards of work, but with many of the accepted ways of doing things.

Why is one wall, constructed over a hundred years ago, still standing, whereas another, only five years old, is crumbling to dust? Why are most gravel paths at National Trust properties and stately homes comfortable to walk on, while a neighbour's recently laid gravel drive is like walking, and driving, through treacle? These and other questions had to be answered if I was to progress. After all, a well-designed garden should be practical as well as a pleasure to be in, regardless of its style or makeup. A wall which slowly disintegrates and a surface which sucks in unsuspecting high heels do not fit these ideals.

My construction expertise, however, was non-existent. In fact, virtually all my attempts at DIY had ended in disaster, and at the time I did not feel qualified to tell others what they were doing wrong. So I set out to make sure that I knew how things should be constructed before specifying them. This involved talking to architects and landscape architects, and reading up on old methods. I concluded that many landscaping problems were a result of late-twentieth-century expediency – many of the tried and tested methods which had been used for centuries were being rejected simply because they took a little more time and some dedication, or because of the attitude that everything we do today is automatically better than the same thing carried out in the past.

Pressure and a lot of persuasion had to be exerted on my recommended contractors to change their way of thinking. At one point this involved me doing backbreaking work on-site to show how I wanted things done. My methods have now been accepted and,

7

where my advice has been adhered to, proved to be correct over the intervening years. It can be difficult for practical reasons to oversee all aspects of a contractor's work, but there are some things to look out for. I shall be looking at these in more detail in Chapter 6.

Costs

The next problem, and one which is constantly raising its ugly head, is that of keeping project costs down. Few people appreciate how much it costs to create a garden from scratch, and those who don't are invariably shocked when they find out. The lion's share of the money goes on the labour costs, not on the materials, mainly for hard structures like walls and paving. There are many ways of reducing the amount of labour required, but the project must be carefully planned in advance; a detailed plan or drawing is essential, not just to inform the contractor, but also for the garden owner to see what he or she is getting.

Despite all the precautions, I soon learnt that it is extremely difficult to create a garden within a set budget. Gardens are living, breathing entities and each requires a different approach. A 1.8 metre (6ft) wide patio may cost less than one 3.5 metres (12ft) wide, but if the garden needs the latter, and only a 6 ft wide one is incorporated, the overall design will be affected. It may not appear to the garden owner at first that there is a problem, but once the garden is in use the shortcomings will quickly become apparent. The best approach is to aim to do the very best job without spending unnecessary money, and, if this exceeds the immediate budget, to create the garden in stages. This is the best approach for every garden maker. It is better to develop one area properly than to

try to spread the available resources too thinly across the whole garden.

Suppliers

The last stage in any garden development is the ordering and planting of the plants. As a newly qualified garden designer I found this the most problematical (and still do). If I had thought the job difficult until now, it was nothing compared to this stage.

My first experience was a garden with over 2,000 plants. They had been ordered from a well-known nursery chain and I had received no indication that there were any problems. I was accompanied by three landscape gardeners who expected to spend the best part of three days planting up. When the order eventually arrived, a high percentage of the plants were missing. Of the rest, a number could not be planted for various reasons (mislabelled, wrong plants or poor quality) and I eventually found myself with less than half the expected plants.

I decided to compile the next client's order myself. This enabled me to experience at first-hand all the problems involved in obtaining the plants for a large plant list. They ranged from plants already promised to me being sold to someone else to plants incorrectly labelled. The worst example of the latter was a batch of forty *Rosa rugosas* labelled as weigela: if someone cannot tell a rose from an ordinary shrub then they are in the wrong business!

The RHS publishes an annual book called *The Plant Finder,* which lists every plant grown in this country and the nurseries that stock it. Before including a plant in your scheme, check it against this book; if it is grown by lots of nurseries then you're probably safe to include it, if not choose a similar plant which is more widely grown.

The education of a busy gardener

A professional gardener needs to know and understand everything about gardens and plants, and that must be his or her ultimate aim. A hobby gardener must also have a thirst for knowledge, but for the busy garden owner, who simply wants a nice garden, it is not necessary. The aim of this book is to concentrate on the important things that a busy gardener needs to know, ignoring what is not necessary and exposing what is flawed.

✿ First, the busy person's approach must be more flexible. Nobody likes uncertainty and gardeners are no exception, so over the decades hard and fast rules have materialized which many gardeners swear by. However, anyone who has a garden knows that it does not grow according to a series of predetermined rules but tends to develop randomly – our approach to gardening should be prepared for this. A plant can be given the very best growing conditions and it will still die; a plant expected to grow to 1.2 metres (4ft) in diameter after eight years can reach that height in two while the same plant next to it has not grown at all. Be prepared for failure, accept it and respond to it –do not waste time being overly concerned.

✿ Be sceptical. If some advice appears illogical, perhaps it is not correct.

✿ Changes to the garden, however tiny, should be investigated thoroughly before they are implemented. For example, incorporating a pond, a vegetable patch, or a greenhouse will significantly add to the workload and should only be considered if you have enough time and interest (see Chapter 9).

✿ Many problems are brought into the garden from elsewhere, often on plants or in their pots – pests and weeds are the most common introductions, but simply buying the wrong plants as the result of a whim can prove disastrous. Plants like snowberry (*Symphoricarpos*), periwinkle (*Vinca major*), which has delightful blue flowers in the spring, and deadnettle (*Lamium*) can be very invasive – they will quickly get a solid grip on the garden and be difficult to eradicate. Check what the future holds for a plant before introducing it. For more details on unwelcome additions, see page 150.

✿ Try to identify the time-consuming aspects of the garden and explore ways of keeping down the amount of work involved. Look at the overall design and see if you can simplify the whole scheme without losing what is best about the garden.

✿ Construction is important. Mistakes made at this stage may not be apparent for a few years, but when they do become so, the problems can be very serious indeed. Choosing and employing a landscape gardener is not easy – you will be placing yourself and the success of the garden in their hands. My advice is to employ someone who comes on a recommendation from a friend or from a dedicated garden designer.

✿ There is nothing to beat thorough preparation. A garden plan will help everyone involved – a garden which develops as it grows may very well turn out to be a delight, but it will involve a lot of work to create and later to maintain. This type of gardening is best left to the hobby gardener.

Chapter 2

Myths and Legends

Although nowadays other eras are better known for their gardens, the Victorians can rightly claim to have been the best gardeners. They developed many techniques for growing plants, not just for the table, but also to impress their friends. It was the time of the great plant hunters, when new discoveries were regularly being brought back from the far reaches of the empire, and gardening developed to make the most of these new plants. There is much to commend what the Victorians achieved, but there are also aspects, especially regarding style, and their use of cheap labour, which are less attractive.

One of the biggest influences on the gardening of the twentieth century was William Robinson, a Victorian himself, who

✿ **Victorian bedding schemes became ever more elaborate – a style of gardening continued in public parks up to the present day.**

creative gardening for busy people

reacted against the contrivances of his era to propose a more natural-looking garden. His book *The English Flower Garden*, published in 1894, is remarkable for being so far ahead of its time and for the way it anticipates the problems of today. Robinson rails against municipal bedding schemes, over-elaborate fountains and balustrades, 'geometrical monotony' and displays a healthy distaste for architects who produce buildings without regard to the gardens. The astounding thing is that much of what he says is as true today as it was then. In fact, I would go as far as to say that in many ways we are still in the Victorian era and are unable, or are reluctant, to break free.

The Victorians achieved many things, but there is a tendency to dismiss much of what is good about their gardening as irrelevant to the late twentieth century and to cling to many of the bad things, such as bedding schemes, rose gardens, rockeries and specimen planting in lawns. It is no coincidence that all these features are high in maintenance, for it was not unusual for each garden to have a vast retinue of gardeners.

Now, however, we are moving into a new millennium and live in an era when time is at a premium. Most people want an attractive, relaxing garden but they do not have the time, nor the inclination, to spend hour after hour maintaining it. This chapter is concerned with exposing some of the myths about gardening, many of which date back more than a hundred years to the time of the Victorians, and suggesting a more modern approach. Something which can genuinely carry the English garden into a new millennium and keep it on the top of the world of horticulture.

30 myths about gardening

1 The only way to grow alpines is on a rockery

This is not true. The term 'alpine' has been corrupted over the years and is now applied to any miniature plant which is not large enough to be put in any other category.

The Victorians invented rockeries at a time when all things natural were in vogue. The idea was to create a natural-looking rock outcrop which could have been in existence for millions of years (a good example can be seen at the Royal Horticultural Society garden at Wisley). Unfortunately, over a period of time this ideal has been corrupted to a pile of soil covered in pieces of rock or even lumps of concrete or clinker, looking more like a plum pudding than a rock outcrop.

See page 99 for alternative ways of displaying alpines.

2 Bedding plants are the best way to introduce colour into the garden

It is true that bedding plants are very colourful, but it is a lot of work to grow, plant and maintain a display throughout a season. In fact there are perennial plants which are just as colourful, easy to grow, and require virtually no effort. See page 114 for more details.

3 Bedding plants are on sale so it must be safe to plant them

The garden will not be completely free of frost until June, and tender bedding plants can still be killed by a frost at any time in May. They are on sale earlier than this because some people like to plant up containers and grow them on under cover before putting them outside. If you want to plant your bedding plants out during May, be prepared to protect them if a frost is forecast. You can cover them with an old net curtain, horticultural fleece (available at any garden centre) or individual plastic flowerpots.

4 The leaves of spring-flowering bulbs must be allowed to die down naturally

This is true. The energy for the flowers in these plants is stored within the bulb and is built up during the previous season, after it has flowered and before it has become dormant. This build-up of stored energy within the bulb is critical, so any interference with the foliage after flowering will affect it. Serious interference over a sustained period will cause the plant to cease flower production.

The answer is to leave the plants alone and let them die down naturally or, at least, wait six weeks before tidying them up. The only thing that you might want to do is remove any seed-heads which will take away energy from the bulb.

For more information on growing bulbs, see page 135.

5 Many herbaceous plants die down to the ground in winter

Yes, they do – some, such as hostas, completely disappear, leaving no trace on the soil surface. Many people throw plants away, especially house or conservatory ones, in the autumn, believing that they personally have been responsible for the plant's demise.

6 The best time to plant is in the autumn

For some plants this is true, but not for all. The theory behind autumn planting is that plants tend to put their energy into root development at this time of year and the ground will still be warm after the summer. In spring the ground has not yet warmed up after the winter and the plant's energy is concentrated on producing top growth. These are very sound and logical reasons for planting in the autumn. The problems come from two very different sources: first, some plants need to have put on a season's growth before facing their first winter or they will simply be killed, or so badly weakened that killing would be a kindness. The other problem results from the mechanics of the horticultural business itself and relates to herbaceous perennials. The highest demand for herbaceous plants is in the spring, when garden centres are stocking up for the coming season. Unlike trees and shrubs, herbaceous perennials have a limited life in containers, tending to be grown fresh every year, and the nurseryman will be aiming to have his new stock ready for the spring rush. This means that herbaceous perennials in the autumn are older plants in quite large containers, and can cost as much as three times the price of a smaller plant in the spring.

The advantages of spring over autumn planting became apparent when comparing gardens planted at these two different times of the year. There has always been a significantly higher number of losses from autumn planting, something borne out by discussions with nurserymen. A factor in this may be that people are more likely to look after plants in the spring and summer.

March or April are good times to plant – and later if you live in an area where hosepipe bans are a rare occurrence. Even June.

If your garden is ready for planting in the autumn, plant only the hardiest varieties of shrubs and climbers and leave all the herbaceous plants and other shrubs until the spring. Roses, most spring bulbs and bare-rooted trees are all best planted in the autumn.

7 Plants require sun to grow

Well... yes. Sunlight is important in photosynthesis, but not all plants require full sun. In fact many plants will not be happy growing in full sun at all.

✿ **This wildflower meadow has been painstakingly recreated for Cartier at the Chelsea Flower Show, but in less than ideal conditions a wildflower garden can be extremely difficult to maintain.**

8 Buy only good-quality plants from a reputable source

There is some logic in this statement, and it is correct to an extent, but there are too many anomalies to make it all-encompassing. Many of the best garden plants suffer in containers, looking poor as a result, and cannot reach their full potential until 'released' into the garden.

The interesting thing is that many plants actually benefit from periodic rough treatment, which is why some roses, buddleias and other deciduous plants are cut hard back every spring. Herbaceous perennials benefit from being dug up every three or four years, hacked into pieces and replanted. All these plants not only recover, but flower better as a result. Turning this on its head, most poor plants will recover and make perfectly good specimens.

Plants kept in containers for long periods can become pot-bound. This condition is identified by a matted root system around the edge of the pot, with roots appearing through the hole in the base. This is not necessarily a problem – the plant will usually grow away quickly as long as the roots are loosened and teased out before planting in a large well-prepared hole. If confronted by a plant in this condition, and if the price is reasonable, you shouldn't be afraid to buy. If, however, the plant is expensive, avoid it. With some plants the condition is unavoidable – they grow quickly and their root system soon fills up any size container.

I am not suggesting that you seek out poor plants, but you should not be too afraid of them. As long as they are deciduous, are planted in the spring and are given some cosseting, you should have no qualms. For more details on buying plants and identifying problems, see Chapter 4.

9 Wildflower gardening is easy and low in maintenance

There is nothing to compare with a field of wildflowers, and their loss through modern farming methods has left our lives much the poorer, but it is wrong to believe that it is easy to recreate the same effect in our own gardens. It is certainly not low in maintenance.

First, most of those we know as meadow flowers grow on impoverished chalkland. In a rich garden soil they grow well, but not as well as the wild plants which are normally found there: plants like dock and nettles will slowly strangle the meadow flowers. On impoverished soil every plant is competing on equal terms.

If you do have the right soil, you must start the scheme off with pot-grown plants. Most of these plants are annuals, so they must be allowed to set and distribute their seed before being cut back. The time of cutting will vary from the middle of July to some time in August, depending upon where the garden is situated. For instance, the wildflower meadow at Great Dixter in Sussex is cut on 17 July every year; as you move further north the cutting day will be later.

As you can imagine, the last four weeks of the process are extremely untidy, so is best done only in a large garden where it can be hidden from sight or absorbed into the landscape. Wildflower gardening is best left to the hobby gardener.

10 Plants should always be planted in groups of three

Only if the plants hold their shape, although I would suggest that planting in odd numbers is a more acceptable rule. It is a curious thing that many garden features look better in odd-

✿ Roses offer so much to the mixed border both in colour and in length of flowering that it is a waste to concentrate them in monoculture beds. **Here** *Rosa* 'Hermosa', *R.* 'New Dawn' **(climbing rambler) combine with** *Lavandula* 'Munstead', *Alchemilla mollis* **and** *Delphinium* 'Black Knight' **with stunning effect.**

numbered groups, and plants are no exception. But if they simply grow into each other to create an indefinable mass, or are part of a hedge, the rule does not apply.

11 Grasses and bamboos are invasive

It took me a number of years to include grasses and bamboos in my designs, as I was afraid of the problems they might cause. In fact, most of these plants are quiet and inoffensive, but the small number of invasive varieties are such a nuisance that they have tainted the reputation of the others.

For more details of invasive plants see page 150.

12 Roses must be grown in dedicated rose beds.

This is a hangover from the past, when roses had a very special, almost regal, position in the garden. Because of its limited season, the rose garden would usually be hidden behind high walls or hedges, to be visited only during the summer months when the roses were at their best. This avoided the need to look at them during the rest of the year, and between visits the gardeners would be working hard, pruning, spraying and feeding to ensure the very best display.

Roses have always had a special place in the garden, which has elevated them above other plants, but in reality they are nothing more than a very diverse group of flowering shrubs. Planting them in monoculture beds is frankly a waste. Many roses will flower for a long period and should be used in conjunction with other plants to create an overall effect. If you still want a dedicated rose bed, why not surround it with a hedge of dwarf lavender, *Lavandula 'Hidcote'*,

incorporating *Hebe rakaiensis* or *H. toparia* at each corner? This will give some winter colour and help to hide the bare soil. Alternatively, hide your rose bed behind a high wall as the Victorians did.

13 Bush roses are high-maintenance

It is true that some roses require judicious pruning and spraying to get the best from them, but generally they require little work. If you avoid hybrid teas, which are grown for their large blooms, you need only remove dead, diseased and dying wood (the three Ds) in March. Dead-heading helps to keep the flowering season going, but for many roses, especially the later developers, even that is not necessary. Some roses are susceptible to disease and these will require spraying, but if you select your variety carefully this can be kept to a minimum. For more details see page 132.

Roses are greedy, however, and appreciate an annual top-dressing of well-rotted manure or compost plus a handful of rose fertilizer in the spring and again in mid-summer to help keep the flowers coming.

14 Roses have to be pruned to just above the ground every spring

Many deciduous shrubs benefit from being cut hard back in the spring, so you won't do any harm, but in most cases it is not necessary. Hybrid tea roses benefit from hard pruning in March, as this encourages the production of better blooms. Other roses need only the three Ds (dead, diseased and dying wood) removed, which again should be done in March, but can also be carried out at any time during the summer or autumn.

15 Roses should not be planted in ground where roses have been growing during the previous four years

This one is not a myth. The roots of roses, or perhaps parasites living on those roots, deposit a chemical into the soil which interferes with the development of other roses, probably to deter competition. It is easily resolved by exchanging the soil with rose-free soil taken from elsewhere in the garden (remove soil to a spade's depth and from 30cm (1ft) either side of main stem). The Royal National Rose Society recommends soaking the soil with Armillatox (available at most garden centres) to control the problem, commonly called rose sickness, but I would only do this in conjunction with the soil replacement.

16 Roses require regular spraying

Yes and no. Many older varieties of hybrid teas and floribundas are prone to a variety of problems and require a fortnightly spray during the growing season, but newly developed roses are required to go through rigorous field trials to weed out those prone to disease. As a general rule, the thicker and more rubbery the leaves, the more resistant to disease they are.

Having said this, in certain conditions even the toughest plant can suffer from mildew and in some years blackspot can be more of a problem than in others. Where the air remains still, perhaps close to a wall, mildew is more likely to develop than in a more open part of the garden.

Unfortunately there are no greenfly-resistant roses. So these have to be dealt with, and this is best done by a systemic insecticide (one which is absorbed through the leaves of the plant and kills any insect which eats the plant).

17 Laburnum is poisonous and should not be planted where children play

The seeds of the laburnum are poisonous – so are the fruits of honeysuckle, the leaves of box and yew, hellebores and numerous other garden plants. In most cases it requires large quantities to do any damage, and these plants do not have a pleasant taste. Children should be taught from an early age not to eat anything that they find in the garden, especially plants. However, there is probably more danger from the garden pond, unattended garden tools or steps.

I must add, however, that monkshood (*Aconitum napellus*) is extremely poisonous and I do not like to see it planted in any garden. A number of house and conservatory plants are also very poisonous (angel's trumpets, oleander and croton, for example) and these represent a much bigger threat.

18 Trees should always be supported by a short stake

After many years of field trials it has been discovered that trees develop better if supported by a short stake, as this allows the plant to sway in the wind and encourages a better root system to develop. So far so good. The problem is that there are still occasions when a full stake is advisable. One is where there is a constant prevailing wind, usually on a hillside, where, if a short stake is used, the tree will grow at an angle caused by the wind. The second is a problem with container-grown trees. Many of these plants have been growing in their containers for several years,

17

often close together, and this can result in a very weak stem which can snap just above a short stake. For more details see page 138.

19 Pot-grown trees are as good as bare-rooted ones.

Doubtful. Before someone invented the disposable flowerpot, all plants had to be purchased either root-balled or bare-rooted and only at certain times of the year. Nowadays we are able to obtain virtually all plants in pots from the garden centre at any time of the year, but this is not necessarily the best way to buy them.

Most deciduous plants can be moved easily during their dormant period – October to March – simply by lifting them from the ground and brushing the soil from the exposed roots. As long as they are not out of the ground for too long and the roots can be kept damp and frost-free, there should be no problem.

A bare-rooted tree has developed in an open ground situation, ensuring a strong tree with a well-developed root system. Compare this to a pot-grown plant which has had its roots restricted, perhaps for several years, and develops a weak brittle trunk on a poor root system.

20 All apples and pears require a pollinator

This is true. A pollinator is simply a different variety of apple or pear that flowers at exactly the same time. Without it the fruit cannot be successfully fertilized. Some trees are sold as being self-fertile: these usually consist of a branch from another variety grafted (joined) on to the main plant. Information on pollinators is best obtained from a specialist nursery, whose catalogues will be up to date and filled with invaluable information. Look in the back of one of the leading gardening magazines for contacts.

21 Always allow a hedge to grow to the height you want before trimming it

There are two schools of thought when it comes to the exact time to start trimming a hedge: one says that the hedge should receive its first cut when it has reached its desired height and the other that it should be trimmed early and allowed to grow to its desired height in a controlled manner.

Personally, I prefer the latter. Creating a small hedge and maintaining it until it reaches the desired height allows problems, like 'gapping' at the base, to be resolved as early as possible, especially with conifers.

22 To have a fine lawn I must mow it as close as possible

In most situations this is what creates problems in a lawn. Cricket wickets, golf greens and bowling greens are cut very close, it is true, but the turf used is much finer and has to be treated this way. With ordinary garden turf, which is probably a mixture of fine and hard-wearing grasses, cutting it too close weakens it so that it cannot compete with weeds and moss. Much better to maintain it at 4 cm (1½ in) or even longer. This approach will thicken the sward and strengthen each grass plant so that it excludes any weeds. For more details see pages 34 and 112.

23 Ants eat greenfly

I am not sure how this myth began, but nothing could be further from the truth.

✿ **There is nothing to be gained from this type of gardening. The plants suffer and the owner must spend more time maintaining it.**

Ants actually farm greenfly ('aphid' is the name given to these sap-sucking insects). By rubbing the aphid's back with their antennae the ant is rewarded with a sweet sticky secretion – a delicacy in the ant world. In fact, ants have been known to transport aphids between plants and even to overwinter them in their nests.

Having said this, I do not recommend that you go on the warpath against the local ant population. They can be a problem in many areas of gardening, but they are also part of the general ecology and, as predators, help to maintain a balance. It would also be a fruitless task trying to eradicate them – a waste of time and resources.

24 Ground-cover plants are low in maintenance

The term 'ground-cover' is given to those plants that are low-growing and form a carpet across the soil. They smother most weeds and therefore reduce weeding. The problem is that they are generally very robust and want to cover a very large area, so what you gain by not having to weed, you lose by having to keep the 'solution' plant under control.

Ground-cover plants certainly have their uses, but require careful investigation before being planted.

✿ **Myth 28. Scalloped edges are difficult to maintain and are not the best way to create informality in the garden.**

25 *Leylandii* **hedges are low in maintenance**

I appreciate that this statement might appear a little strange, but these conifers are planted by people who want an instant screen and an easy life. The fact is that the faster a plant grows the more tending it requires and, of course, *Cupressocyparis leylandii* is one of the fastest growing.

26 **For a low-maintenance garden I must plant shrubs and avoid herbaceous perennials**

I suppose that, on balance, there are more trouble-free shrubs than trouble-free herbaceous perennials, but that is not the whole story. In fact, many of the latter require no work at all, exclude weeds and flower for a long period.

27 **Growing plants in the lawn is a low-maintenance solution**

It is strange how this practice has developed in recent years, against a torrent of advice to the contrary. Grass takes a lot of moisture and goodness from the soil and will impede the growth of any plant grown in it. It will also be much more difficult to mow the lawn. This is far from a low-maintenance solution.

28 **Straight lines and evenly spaced plants are too formal**

The danger here is that the garden owner becomes too obsessed with curves at the expense of common sense. Curves in paving often involve a lot of cutting, making the project costly and impractical, and the final result is not necessarily informal. Practical lines, straight or at an angle, can be softened by allowing plants to cascade over the edges; this will create informality much more effectively.

Within a planting scheme it is a good idea to repeat the same plant at intervals throughout, as this gives balance and continuity. The eye feels comfortable with this balance and it should not be confused with formality.

29 **Every garden needs a strimmer**

With some careful thought it is possible to remove the need for a strimmer for normal work in the garden. If you think about it, a strimmer is only required where the lawn butts up against a vertical surface – a fence, tree, wall, etc. Cut the turf back from that vertical surface and fill the newly created space with gravel, bark mulch or plants and you will need only a mower.

The strimmer is the scythe of the modern age and, as such, is invaluable for clearing overgrown areas.

30 **No garden is complete without a compost heap**

The problem is that most compost heaps consist of a circle of chicken wire tucked away in the corner of the garden, which becomes nothing more than a deposit for garden rubbish. This rubbish consists mainly of grass cuttings, and the term 'compost' is just an excuse to hide what is a tip.

Making usable compost is fairly involved and needs a degree of work and dedication to be effective. If that dedication is not forthcoming, what is produced will do more harm than good.

For more details on successful composting see page 111.

21

Chapter 3

Designing the Garden

For a garden to function smoothly and be successful, proper foundations must be laid down at the outset and this can only be achieved if a plan of action is devised and drawn up. Even without the skills of a garden designer, this is a much better approach than allowing the garden to develop haphazardly over a period. It enables time for reflection, time to decide what is really wanted and for elements of the garden to be placed in a more logical fashion than if each is developed in isolation.

If you make a plan, the garden can be developed over a number of years, but this does not mean that the design is set in stone. It can be modified as circumstances and desires alter, but in a controlled manner, avoiding rash and ill-thought-out decisions.

A plan also enables everyone in the family to contribute to the new garden.

The art of garden design is an area of horticulture that is much maligned and misunderstood, but it can be invaluable to those who want an easy garden. Professional garden designers deal constantly with clients who want an instant garden with the minimal amount of work, and they have developed techniques to help them achieve this.

The first thing to realize about garden design is that show gardens, including those at the main Royal Horticultural Society shows, are, in general, not good examples. The need to cram both plants and the sponsor's wares into what is essentially a small space often creates designs that are impractical and unworkable. Some designers

✿ **Show gardens are often extremely congested, making the design impractical for the average garden.**

believe that the show garden is to the garden designer what the catwalk is to the fashion designer – in other words the show garden should not be taken too seriously. Sadly, this rather irresponsible attitude has not reached the thousands of visitors each year armed with their notebooks and pens.

This does not mean that show gardens cannot be learnt from – many individual ideas within the gardens can inspire and can be modified for use in other settings. An innovative water feature, a garden seat or even a new way of using containers may stir the imagination, but the overall designs are best ignored.

What the busy garden owner needs is a plan which is achievable, both physically and financially, something which is going to give pleasure without the need for excess work and which can be carried out quickly and painlessly. To achieve this, follow the same steps taken by the professionals.

✿ **This close-up of the garden shown earlier highlights a fine brick waterfall, something which could easily be included in a private garden.**

Analysing the garden

First take some notes. Decide what you would like to incorporate in the garden. This could include statues, a water feature, somewhere to sit, a garden shed, a greenhouse – and don't forget mundane things like a clothes drier. A garden should 'breathe', so the best designs are the simplest – adding too many features, particularly in a small garden, will close it up and make it feel claustrophobic. Each item will also have a financial impact. Think about how you

intend to use the garden. Barbecuing and entertaining may mean a larger patio, and football with the children will certainly involve a larger lawn.

Once you have made a list of what you would like to incorporate, the next stage is to look closely at the existing garden. Identify problem areas and those areas which you would like to change. You should also identify the good points and those areas that please you most.

Now draw a rough plan. Work out where the sun rises and sets; this sounds simple, but some people, even those who have lived with a garden for a number of years, do not know which way their garden faces. The easiest method is to use a compass.

Mark on your plan any permanent features, such as trees, garden buildings, ponds, which you intend to keep in the new design. You should also include features outside the boundary. In fact, do not ignore the environment beyond the garden, as it

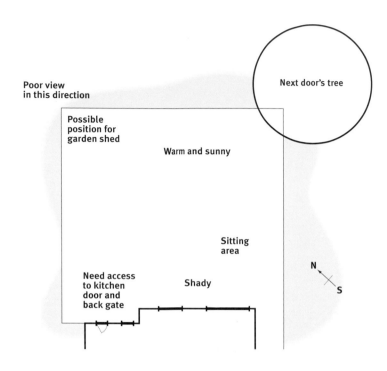

Poor view
in this direction

Possible
position for
garden shed

Warm and sunny

Next door's tree

Sitting
area

Need access
to kitchen
door and
back gate

Shady

N

S

A sitting area

Usually a paved area or patio close to the house or, in a north-facing shady garden, a sunny spot away from the house. One word of warning: sitting areas remote from the house are generally under-used, as they are too far from facilities. In a north-facing garden it is much better to develop two areas, the remote one in the sunny spot and a main one close to the house.

Lawn

Most gardens will include an area of lawn. True, it is top of the maintenance league table, but it can be difficult to find a suitable alternative surface without the use of extensive paving, which can be harsh and pricey. Grass is one of the least expensive surfaces and a lawn can be a cool relaxing place to sit on a hot day. Obviously there are occasions when it is not appropriate, but think long and hard before omitting it.

Outbuildings:
sheds and greenhouses

If you feel the buildings will be heavily used, especially in winter, it may be sensible to introduce an access path. This path should be as practical as possible – avoid stepping stones, which are really only visual features

> ✿ **A rough drawing will help you to analyse and assess your garden, identifying its good and bad points before producing a design.**

probably has some kind of impact; perhaps there is a large tree casting shadow, or a noisy children's playground. Identify any good or bad views; include any sources of noise pollution.

This exercise will also force you to look closely at your garden and make more informed decisions, perhaps even resulting in the removal of items from the notes taken earlier. Once this part of the analysis plan has been completed, start to work out the best places in the garden for the features listed in the notes. In most cases the list will include some or all of the following items.

and impossible to push a wheelbarrow along. Make sure that the path is wide enough for your needs.

A gazebo or summerhouse.

Gazebo is a word which has developed from the term 'gaze about' and traditionally described a small, six- or eight-sided garden building with three or four of the sides closed off and the others open. There are many different designs on the market, a large number of which do not bear any resemblance to the traditional design described above.

A summerhouse is a small garden building similar to a gazebo, but part-glazed. There are no traditional shapes for a summerhouse – they can just as easily be rectangular as octagonal. One warning: before installing one, ensure that it is actually going to be used for what you intend – all too often these buildings become store rooms for deckchairs and barbecues. This is often the result of the building being too small in the first place, so make sure you choose a good size.

These garden structures can be very pricey, so think carefully before buying. They are very useful as focal points, in the same way that a garden seat can be, but they can dominate a small garden. It may be that a garden seat under a pergola or arbour would achieve what is required, but with less cost.

✿ **The dimensions of a gazebo or summerhouse should feel comfortable. Too much pitch in the roof and it begins to look awkward. This summerhouse (remove the glass, open it up and it will be transformed into a gazebo) is perfectly proportioned.**

Water features

There is a closer study of water features in Chapter 9. However, at the design stage the positioning is critical. If a large natural pond is to be incorporated, it should ideally be sited in the lowest part of the garden, where a pond could be expected to develop naturally. This should only be attempted in a garden large enough to accommodate it – in a small garden there are many alternative ways of introducing water. As most activity in and around a water feature takes place in the spring (e.g. frogs spawning, plants blooming), I recommend that it is sited where it can best be enjoyed at that time of year. This is usually close to the house or a frequently used pathway – between the patio and the rest of the garden is usually best, where it can be seen from the kitchen or lounge windows.

Clothes drier

For the perfect garden, dry your clothes in a tumble drier! Of course this is not generally practical, and a garden must be functional as well as a place to play. There are two types of drier, the rotary and the line – choose whichever fits best with the new design. The former takes up less space but, despite our best efforts, tends to be left out when not in use. The latter is perhaps the most garden-friendly and, I am told, more effective. If you buy the type with a spring-loaded reel, the line can be easily retracted when not in use. Although ideal visually, the line can be very difficult to fit into a design because the user needs a solid path to stand on when loading – this paving must run the length of the line, which usually excludes it from use.

My recommendation is to leave the decision of which method to use until the design has been completed. If a line can be installed over the paving within the design, fine, if not then position a rotary drier in the lawn just off the patio. Try to avoid designing the garden around the clothes drier.

Other features can also

be plotted at this stage, but they are more likely to be moved around as the design develops and their ideal position becomes clearer. Make a note of them. The completed analysis drawing will form the basis of the new garden, but before we can look at the overall design, we must make some more decisions.

Style and surroundings

Some people's answer to the problems of the garden is to throw money at it – often large amounts. Classical fountains, balustrades, Venus de Milo style statues and large stretches of water can all be combined to create something which looks more like a cemetery than a garden. I have visited many private

✿ Features such as classical fountains need the correct setting if they are not to become an eyesore. Here the desire for a classical fountain came first, and deciding whether the garden was an appropriate setting for it a distant second.

gardens which have had vast amounts of time and money lavished upon them, and the result has an uncomfortable feel – as if you must perch on the edge of your seat instead of sitting back and relaxing. These gardens tend to develop from one person's obsession, without an integrated plan.

In most cases the problem is caused by the overall style sitting awkwardly within the garden in which it has been created. The key to avoiding this is to look at the garden within its setting, in other words the style of the house and surrounding countryside. For instance, a garden attached to a thatched cottage will look good as long as the design is understated and includes the soft planting used in a traditional cottage garden. One of the best hard surfaces for this type of garden is pea shingle, which is, coincidentally, also one of the least expensive. It is important to understand that the perfect garden is not necessarily the most expensive one.

If the garden is surrounded by countryside, incorporate some of the local country plants – perhaps some hawthorn, or a field maple. This will help to settle the new garden into its surroundings.

Having said this, most houses do not suggest any particular style, for example on a suburban estate, where the house is more utilitarian. In these instances, try not to introduce any style at all. Stick with plain paving, perhaps brightened by the addition of bricks to match those used in the house (see Chapter 6), and use copious mixed planting to smooth any hard edges.

Another exception to the rule is the theme garden. It is doubtful, for instance, that Japanese gardens would exist outside Japan if the above rules were followed to the letter. The chosen theme, however, must be followed right through the design, if it is to be successful.

A basic design for a small garden

The easiest way to explain the techniques used by a designer is to show the design of a garden from scratch. This small garden could come from any new estate, and is perhaps the most common size and shape.

The usual approach by a new garden owner is to lay the garden to lawn, create a

✿ **Narrow borders make life very difficult when the gardener is trying to achieve a pleasing effect.**

27

Plan 1

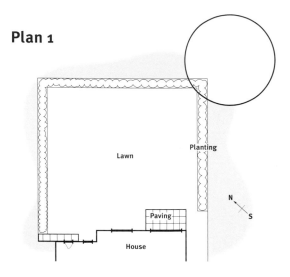

Lawn

Planting

Paving

House

N
S

✿ **A common approach to a new garden is to install a narrow bed around the perimeter in order to maintain as large a lawn area as possible.**

Plan 2

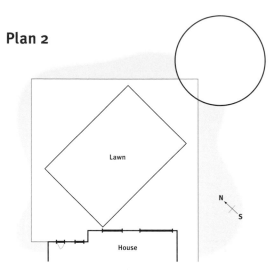

Lawn

House

N
S

✿ **A diamond-shaped lawn offers more potential.**

narrow bed around the perimeter and install a rectangular patio against the house (see Plan 1). This is usually dictated by the desire to make the lawn as large as possible, either for the children or because the owner believes that grass is low-maintenance. The main problem with this is that most shrubs are as wide as they are high and need more space to grow than the thin strip allows. We cannot make a small garden physically larger, but we can use techniques that give a feeling of more space. One of these is to hide the perimeter with plants, preferably with a variety of heights and depths, and to do this we must devise a way of creating the space necessary for the plants we want to include.

The narrow bed around the edge is in fact created by placing a rectangular lawn within a rectangular boundary. Increasing the size of the bed around the edge in a small

garden is not a practical solution, so we must approach the garden in a different way. First, let's change the angles within the garden by changing the lawn to a diamond shape (see Plan 2). This retains the size of the lawn for those who require space for play, but creates larger planting areas in the corners.

The main sitting area is best positioned next to the house, beside the patio door. This paved area, or patio, will fit nicely between the lawn and the house (see Plan 3). This angle on the patio also has the advantage of moving the sitting area down the garden a little away from the house, which may, depending on the aspect, draw it into a sunnier spot.

The change also alters the way we look at the garden. The new angle means that we can view the garden with fresh eyes, no longer restricted by the up-down, side-to-side approach forced on us by the rectangle-

Plan 3

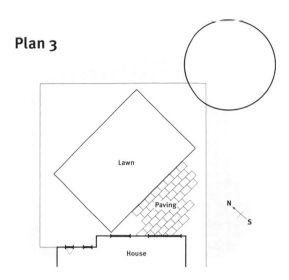

✿ **Add a paved area next to the house.**

✿ **A 'lean-to' pergola is perfect for creating some shade against a south-facing wall.**

within-a-rectangle design. Now that we can 'see' more clearly, the site analysis sketch shows that the view from the new patio is now towards the poor view to the north. Something is needed opposite the patio as a focal point to draw the eye and take attention away from the view.

The pergola

We need height in the north corner. A tree will provide this given time, and it will also balance up the tree beyond the boundary to the east. However, if we want instant screening we must find an alternative.

Pergolas are structures that look like the 'bones' of a tunnel, with a series of interconnected arches. They are usually made of wood, but can be made of brick with wooden cross-beams, concrete, natural stone or wrought iron. They have a number of uses,

but the most common are the 'sit under' and the more traditional 'walk through'. The first is constructed as if it were a skeletal building to be entered from one of the longest sides. It can have one side supported by a wall, and in this way can be very useful in a garden where the sitting area close to the house faces south and requires shade.

The second type of pergola is a free-standing version which straddles a path or route around the garden. The path and the overhead beams tend to draw the eye ahead, so a focal point of some kind, perhaps a seat, or a statue, at either end, will act as a full stop and add purpose.

Pergolas also have good screening properties and can be used in a small garden to draw the eye away from a poor view. A pergola may not obliterate a view totally, but by choosing bold-coloured

✿ **As well as creating a pleasant place to sit or walk, the overhead growth on a pergola can make pleasing and interesting patterns on the ground.**

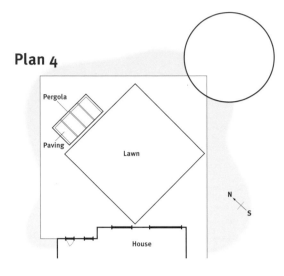

Plan 4

Pergola

Paving

Lawn

House

N

S

✿ **A pergola creates an eye-catching focal point.**

plants to grow on it, the eye can be drawn away from the eyesore.

In our sample garden, a 'sit under' pergola will make a good screen in the north corner (see Plan 4). It isn't very big and will make a useful frame for a garden seat, placed to create an eye-catching focal point, as well as being somewhere to sit and enjoy the garden.

Illusions

Good design can make a small garden appear larger, but the reverse is also true – bad design can make a garden appear even smaller. There are three ways to give the illusion of more space:

1 Hiding the edges, although probably reducing the amount of physical space, gives the illusion that the garden is unrestricted and endless. I want to make a quick mention of hedges here, as around a small garden they can be a disaster. They make it impossible to hide the perimeter, as the hedge becomes the perimeter. They can reduce the size of the garden by as much as 1.5 metres (5 ft), as it is not just the amount of space taken up by the hedge, it is also the amount of space next to it where nothing will grow and which has to be left for maintenance.

2 Designing the garden so that the whole of it cannot be seen in one glimpse usually involves splitting the garden up into 'rooms', but to do this in a small garden is both impractical and in many cases impossible. The answer is to cheat. Imagine somebody visiting the garden for the first time. Our task is to persuade them that they want to walk around the garden – not to stand and stare, but to explore.

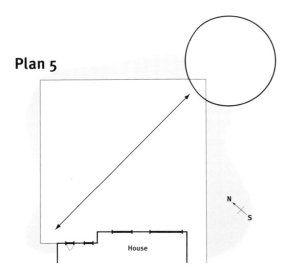

Plan 5

House

Plan 6

Pergola

Paving

Lawn

Patio

House

✿ The longest line in the garden runs diagonally from corner to corner.

✿ Running the lines within the design diagonally creates a feeling of space.

In a large garden, the designer would link the 'rooms' with strategically placed paths so that no matter where our visitor was in the garden, they would be aware that there was still more garden to explore. In a small garden this effect can be created by setting up dummy 'rooms' that do not exist. This can be done by making an arch in the taller planting and perhaps emphasizing it by introducing a path leading to it. The path and arch could lead to a compost heap or storage area, or even to a statue or urn sited as a focal point.

Another technique in a small garden is to alter the view from the house, so that there is a different vista from each downstairs window. This can be achieved by introducing a planted area in the centre of the garden close to the house. It will give depth to the garden as well as altering the views.

3 The longest line in the garden is the one running diagonally from corner to corner, and if we can emphasize this imaginary line we can 'push' out the corners, giving the illusion of more space (see Plan 5). In our sample garden, another advantage of the diagonal patio can now be seen, as it emphasizes the line from corner to corner. This 'line' can be further built upon by running the pattern in the paving diagonally as well (see Plan 6).

The patio

A mistake many people make is to create a patio area that is far too small. A patio needs to have space enough to move around easily. Make sure it is at least large enough for a reasonable size table and four chairs, allowing enough space around the edge for the chairs to be moved backwards as guests stand up and move around. Finally, allow a further 60 cm (2 ft) near planted areas for plants to grow over the paving.

Try not to make the area too large – over-large patios come across as harsh and unwelcoming and also represent money that could be better spent elsewhere.

Cost can be a factor in any design, but there are ways of keeping it to a minimum. The lion's share of the finance goes on labour charges, so if we can reduce the amount of work required, the costs will also fall. One high cost involves the cutting of paving material, something that with some thought can be kept to a minimum. Initially, the decision to run the paving diagonally in the sample garden looks like an expensive option, but, by cutting the paving slabs only where absolutely necessary, where the patio butts up against a door or pathway, the cost can be brought down. This approach also creates planted areas close to the house and the irregular pattern around the edges can be varied for effect.

In our sample garden, the patio shows how effective and flexible the paving pattern can be. Note that the only place where the paving needs to be cut is beside the patio door.

Paths

Many paths become unusable or unsightly after a while. With some thought and careful design, there is no reason why a path cannot enhance the garden, in the same way as a pergola or pond.

Paths must be made wide enough, be constructed soundly and have a purpose. Ignoring these three rules will store up problems for the future. Ideally, a path should be wide enough for two people to walk along side by side comfortably. Beside a planted area plants can be allowed to tumble over it, thereby softening the path, but space must be allowed to accommodate this, otherwise the effect will be spoiled by the need to continually cut back the plants. I have visited gardens where the path has completely vanished under encroaching foliage. 1.2 metres (4ft) is a good width, although in a large garden a path could be made even wider.

There are many different surfaces that can be used for a path, but whatever the choice it should be flat, comfortable and practical in use. Read Chapter 6 before coming to a final decision. Stepping stones in a lawn are a common choice, but should be used with care. Visually they can be effective, perhaps comprising a short path leading to a garden seat, but they are uncomfortable to walk on, mainly because everyone's gait is different. They are also impractical, as they are almost impossible to negotiate with a wheelbarrow or pushchair.

A path laid in a complicated shape can create problems. If there are tight curves, the material used must be selected carefully. The tighter the curve the smaller the building material, the smallest being pea gravel. Larger paving slabs require very skilful cutting in order to negotiate a tight curve.

Paths should lead somewhere. They should either have a direct purpose, such as leading to a garden seat or building, or complete a circuit around the whole garden, or part of it. Sometimes a design looks better with a path, and a purpose can be created by installing a garden seat, statue or urn for it to lead to.

Earlier, we discussed the illusions that can be created by playing with the lines in the

❁ **Running the line of the brick away from the user adds speed and urgency to the path, guiding people quickly to their destination. Here the path has been designed to lead visitors around the conservatory on the left to the main entrance to the house.**

garden. The pattern in which paving is laid can have a similar effect by altering the character of a path, making the user speed up or slow down. Running the pattern away from the user gives a feeling of speed and purpose to the path. The user is drawn along it with some urgency to reach the end. This can be useful when it is necessary to manipulate the user into taking a certain path or to lead them quickly through an area. It is not relaxed and should be used with care. Running the paving from side to side gives a more relaxed feeling. The user is invited to take his or her time, perhaps stopping to smell the flowers. Confronted with two paths, one of each pattern, a garden user is likely to take the fast route.

Returning to our sample garden, the design so far has incorporated two features, the patios, which are isolated and need linking together. There is also no sound route from the kitchen door. Paths to link the areas have now been inserted – they are of a practical size and fit with the existing style, the irregular edges reducing the amount of slab cutting required (see Plan 7).

The lawn

Many non-gardeners feel that a lawn will need too much maintenance and seek to replace it with paving and gravel, yet a garden with no lawn can be a soulless place. True, cutting the lawn once a week can be time-consuming, but with some careful thought and design at the outset, the work can be kept to a minimum.

Plan 7

Pergola
Paving
Lawn
Paving
N
S
House

❁ **Linking the features and doorways makes the new design practical and easy to use.**

33

✿ **A mowing strip is the best way to retain the shape of a lawn as well as aiding maintenance.**

The first consideration is to keep the lawn area open and uncluttered. Think of how to make it easy to move the lawnmower around. Where possible avoid having anything, such as trees or flower beds, embedded within it. Although the overall shape can be as amoebic as you want, any curves should be big and bold; little squiggles along lawn edges are difficult to maintain and will not create the informality the garden maker sets out to achieve. Informality is best achieved by allowing plants to cascade over the edges. This may of course kill off part of the lawn, but there is something that we can add to avoid this – a mowing strip. This effective little device is the garden designer's gift to the horticultural world. It serves three purposes:

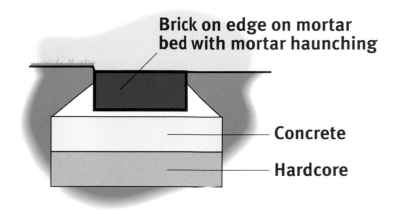

**Brick on edge on mortar
bed with mortar haunching**

Concrete

Hardcore

✿ **The mowing strip: sectional drawing.**

A mowing strip can be made of any of a number of different materials: brick, paving slabs, railway sleepers. Your selection should be based on suitability, style and hardness. Suitability should be based on the design of the lawn – if you have curves look at smaller units, such as brick on edge, as this will enable the mowing strip to negotiate the bends without the need for excessive cutting or cement to cover any gaps. The material selected can affect the overall style of the garden – I would recommend using material that picks out something from the house, such as the colour of the bricks. Whatever material is chosen, it must be hard enough to withstand frost damage. This sometimes means that you cannot always use your first choice, but must find a suitable alternative which is a close match.

The installation is also important. Ideally a mowing strip should be constructed as if it were a very low wall, with a proper foundation – however, as it is not a path to be walked on, it is possible to embed the mowing strip straight into the soil, as long as the soil has good clay content. The best material for this would be either bricks or pavers.

Before making any final decisions, read Chapter 6.

1 It maintains the shape of the lawn, something which is essential if the lawn design is to be more than a simple rectangle. A shape can soon disappear if the edge is constantly being maintained by the gardener.

2 It makes the lawn easier to mow. As long as the lawn has been laid so that it is 1 cm (⅓ in) higher than the mowing strip, the lawnmower will simply skim over the top. This will avoid the need for a strimmer (in fact where lawn meets any paved surface, it should be laid 1 cm (⅓ in) higher).

3 It allows the plants in the border to cascade over the edge and soften the edges, without interfering with the mower or damaging the lawn.

35

Plan 8

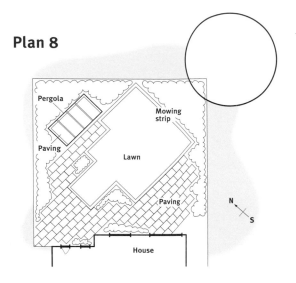

Pergola

Mowing strip

Paving

Lawn

Paving

N
S

House

❀ **The final design.**

Plan 9

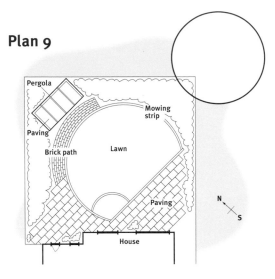

Pergola

Mowing strip

Paving

Lawn

Brick path

Paving

N
S

House

❀ **A semi-circular lawn creates the same amount of space.**

The finished design

Although it is doubtful that it would win any prizes, this simple design would be effective, with some modifications, in almost any small new garden (see Plan 8).

As a variation, the diamond shape could be replaced by a circular design, without affecting the overall plan (see Plan 9). Note that brick has replaced the paving leading to the pergola. This is because smaller units negotiate curves better than larger ones. Whatever shape or size garden you have, create a design on paper before you start developing it. This will enable you to think everything out carefully. Consider the following:

❀ Make sure that any paths or patios are of sufficient size to accommodate your

needs. Is there a natural route through the garden, perhaps to a shed or garage? If so, should you install a path? Whatever you decide to include in your garden, ask yourself whether it will be used, whether it can be easily constructed and whether it will work as you plan it to.

❀ Are you making good use of any views, or should you consider hiding them?

❀ Have you incorporated elements of mystery to draw the visitor out into the garden and give a feeling of more space?

❀ Does the style of the new garden fit well with the house and the surrounding environment?

❀ Is it affordable? Are you spending money unnecessarily?

Chapter 4
Plants

Most of the problems we have with our gardens can be traced back to the plants that are growing there. If we didn't have grass or hedging we wouldn't need to get the lawnmower or hedge-trimmer out of the shed. If we didn't have flower beds, there would be less scope for weeds to develop.

Plants are also complex and difficult to understand. 'Are they getting enough water?' 'Do they need feeding?' 'Why are they covered in brown spots?' 'Why are they dying?' 'Should I be talking to them?' For something that gives so much pleasure, plants can be such a worry. But where would our gardens be without them?

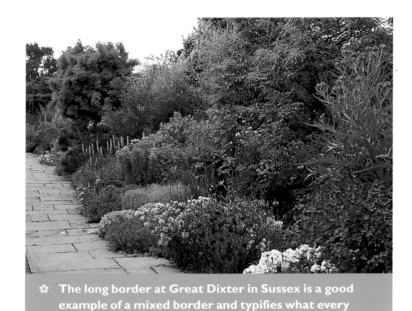

✿ **The long border at Great Dixter in Sussex is a good example of a mixed border and typifies what every garden owner is looking for from a planting scheme.**

I often hear people joke that they would like to concrete over their garden and paint on some grass, or even incorporate plastic turf. True, the garden would be easy to maintain, requiring only occasional sweeping and dusting, but think of what would be lost. No scents, textures or colour. Nothing to mark the changing seasons. Just a sterile landscape of cold hard surfaces. No, gardens were invented for plants and, despite their problems, a garden is not a garden without them. So if we want a pleasant garden we must make some sacrifices and be prepared for some maintenance. To be honest, the more work that we do, the better the garden will be, but that doesn't mean that we need to become a slave to it. With careful selection, most plants in the garden will look after themselves, leaving plenty of time to work on our special favourites.

My dealings with garden owners over the years have thrown up some unusual stories, making it clear that there is a great deal of ignorance about plants and how they behave. One client pointed me at a patch of soil that a landscape gardener had claimed to have filled with a range of plants. The landscaper had said, on completion, that the plants would appear during the following spring, as it was then winter and the plants had died down. When I arrived on the scene, some eighteen months later, the soil was still bare, apart from a smattering of weeds, and a closer inspection of the landscaper's list of plants that he had claimed to have planted revealed roses, weigelas and forsythia among a host of garden plants. He had in fact planted nothing and the client had paid several hundred pounds for this service!

On two other occasions, several years apart, I received calls from clients complaining that many of the plants in their newly planted garden had died and what was I going to do about it? On closer inspection, it turned out that the offending plants were deciduous, and the loss of their leaves was a perfectly natural occurrence.

These cases are extreme, but it shows clearly that there are shortcomings in basic horticultural knowledge. The information in this chapter is designed not to redress the imbalance but to highlight areas of concern and enable the garden owner to make better-informed and considered decisions.

How large will a plant grow?

Perhaps the most common, and potentially the biggest, mistake any gardener can make is in planting a plant which is too large for the amount of space available. I don't mean the height that a plant will grow to, although this can be important, but the amount of space it takes up spreading sideways – a characteristic far more relevant to the garden maker. After all, there is usually plenty of space vertically, but often little sideways.

Garden centres and nurseries tend to concentrate on supplying information on the height of a plant and it can be difficult to find details of the spread. Beware also of the term 'dwarf and low-growing', as some of the biggest monsters are hidden under this banner. Plants like *Juniperus x media* 'Pfitzeriana' or *J. horizontalis* are comparatively low-growing, but their spread can be devastating.

Another area in which to step warily is the rock garden or rockery. Alpines tend to come in two groups – small non-aggressive

✿ **Many conifers sold as dwarf and low-growing are nothing of the sort. Here, two specimens of the common** *Juniperus x media* **'Pfitzeriana' show just how large they really can be. These plants are less than ten years old.**

and low-growing aggressive. A mixture will result in the death of the former and a battle for supremacy between the latter varieties. There are many ways of growing alpines and your selection of rock plant will very much depend on which way you choose (see page 99). In tufa rock or in a small stone sink, for instance, the plants have to be tiny, but in a scree bed, or in paving, large mat-forming alpines are perfect for covering and softening hard surfaces.

When drawing up a planting scheme (I always recommend building the plan up on paper first), a decision must be made as to when the garden is going to reach maturity. Buying plants on a whim at the garden centre, without due thought or consideration, is always a recipe for disaster. But we have all done it and will continue to do so, regardless of the advice in this book. The best thing to do, if you are tempted by a plant, is to go to the book section (most garden centres now have these) and do some on-the-spot investigation before buying. Make sure that it is the right plant for your garden and remember, many people have been undone by a pretty face!

Finally, no plant grows to a set size and then stops – even the most ancient oak puts on some growth every season. This means that at some time in the future the plants in your garden will have exceeded their allocated space and the garden will then start to deteriorate. Some intervention will be required at this stage, either piecemeal, perhaps removing the odd plant, or wholesale, involving a new design.

In the plant lists later in the book I have shown the size that single specimens will reach after approximately eight years, a timescale acceptable to most people.

✿ **Many shrubs, like this** *Cotinus coggygria* **'Grace', form growth which smothers the ground, as long as the conditions are right. I call this ground-covering growth the plant's 'skirt'.**

Ground-cover plants

Ground-cover plants are generally thought of as plants that hug the ground and smother weeds. However, many larger shrubs are natural ground-smotherers, bringing their branches right down to the ground to cover the soil. I like to refer to this ground-covering growth as the plant's 'skirt', and it can be encouraged in some plants by pruning out the leading or top growth. Plants which will not develop a 'skirt' can usually be identified by their shape, which can best be described as an 'ice-cream cone'.

The Latin names

One of the frightening aspects of horticulture for many people is the long Latin names attached to the plants. These are, however, critical descriptions and differentiate one plant from another. Without using the correct name on a plant order it cannot be guaranteed that the expected plant will show up. I like to think of the Latin name as a code, perhaps like a telephone number or a web-site

✿ *Philadelphus* **'Manteau d'Hermine' is a diminutive mock orange.**

address on the Internet – one number or digit out of place and you will either not get through or be directed to the wrong person or computer. Certainly, no one can say that a Latin plant name is more difficult than a web-site address!

Common names are easier to remember, but they are too general and may be attached to a number of different plants. For instance, 'mock orange' is a name attached to a battery of different plants, ranging from the diminutive *Philadelphus* 'Manteau d'Hermine' (growing to 90cm (3ft) in height) to the enormous *P*. 'Virginal' (perhaps 4 m (13ft) in height). Simply asking for 'mock orange' is too much of a gamble.

The Latin names can be useful for finding out some facts about a plant, so

learning something about their makeup is worthwhile and may make them easier to use, or even remember. They were originally invented by a man called Carl von Linné, or Linnaeus, a Swede who lived in the first part of the eighteenth century, to enable scientists to label not just plants, but all living things, properly. The same plant might be known by many different names throughout the world, which made it difficult to communicate internationally. The only answer was an internationally recognized code, and Linnaeus invented it.

Each name carries a description; the genus (*Rosa*, *Philadelphus*, etc.) always comes first in the name and always has a capital letter – think of it as the surname. The following names (think of these as the first, or given names, and there can be several), are (a) a description of the discoverer, as in *Buddleia davidii*; (b) a tribute to someone, as in *Hebe* 'Mrs Winder'; (c) where the plant was discovered, as in *Prunus lusitanica*; (d) a technical description of a prominent part of the plant's makeup, as in *Geranium*

✿ *Philadelphus* **'Virginal' is a mock orange suitable only for the large garden.**

macrorrhizum (meaning 'Big Root'), or (e) habit, as in *Juniperus communis* 'Prostrata' (meaning prostrate-growing). The last can be extremely useful when deciding what impact the plant will have in your garden. Here are some useful descriptions and what they mean:

alba	white
angustifolia	narrow-leafed
arguta	sharply toothed – usually the leaves
atropurpurea, purpurea	purple
caespitosa	tufted
chrysocoma	yellow-haired
compactum	compact
contorta	twisted
cordata/cordifolia	heart-shaped – usually the leaves
cuprea	coppery
dentata	toothed
erecta	erect/ upright

fastigiata	with upright branches
flava	yellow
floribunda	flowering profusely
formosa	beautiful
fragrantissima	very fragrant
fruticosa	shrubby
gigantea	very large
glutinosa	sticky
grandiflora	large-flowered
graveolens	strong-smelling
griseum	grey
horizontalis	growing habit
humilis	low-growing
japonica	from Japan
lanceolatum	lance-shaped leaves
latifolius	broad-leafed
macrophylla	large-leafed
macrorrhizum	with a large root
maculata	spotted
major	larger
microphylla	small-leafed
mollis	soft – may be the leaves or hairs on the leaves
nana, nanum	dwarf
nitida	shiny
nudiflorum	flowers naked (when it is leafless i.e. winter)
odorata	scented
officinalis/ officinale	sold as a herb
palmatum	hand-like – usually the leaves
pictum	painted – usually the look of the leaves
procumbens	prostrate
prostrata	prostrate
pseudo	false (as in *Robinia pseudoacacia* – false acacia)
pumila	dwarf, low-growing
pungens	spiny, sharp-pointed
pyramidalis	pyramid-shaped

radicans	with rooting stems
repanda,	
repandens	creeping
roseum	rose-coloured
rubrifolia	red
sempervirens	evergreen
serpens	creeping
spinosus	spiny
squamata	flaky
tinctoria	used in dyeing
tuberosus	tuber-rooted
undulatum	wavy-edged
variegata	variegated – usually the foliage
verruculosa	with small warts
vulgaris	common

Always copy the Latin name out in full when ordering the plants; being as accurate as possible will show the nurseryman that you mean business. It will also avoid confusion. If in doubt, obtain a copy of the Royal Horticultural Society's *The Plant Finder* (see page 157).

Rose breeders' names

Because of the vast numbers of roses available and the many more which appear each year, it became necessary to develop a separate international code. Many names are devised for marketing purposes, and a name which is effective in one country may not be as effective in another. For instance, *Rosa* 'Angela Rippon' would have little relevance anywhere other than in the United Kingdom, so in another country it will be allocated a more appropriate name. To stop confusion, each rose breeder attaches a name to a rose which stays with it whichever country it is grown in. For example, the breeder's name for *R*. 'Savoy Hotel' is Harvintage and for *R*.

'Gertrude Jekyll' is Ausbord. The first three letters represent the breeder's name – in these cases the first rose was developed by Harkness Roses and the second by David Austin.

As far as you and I are concerned, these codes are useful if we see a rose that we like in another country and would like to obtain it when we return home. Breeders' names did not appear until 1979, so anything bred before this date will not have one attached.

The suitability of a plant

Plants are generally very specific about their requirements. Some like it hot where others like it cold, some like damp soil, others dry, some like acid soil, others alkaline and so on. They come from many different environments, some from the far reaches of the world. In all these places they actually choose to grow there. Here, we are expecting them to grow in what to them is an alien environment, which many would not have chosen. We must therefore try to simulate their preferred conditions as closely as possible.

The following sections will look at those critical conditions.

Sun or shade?

Do not fall into the trap which says that all plants require full sun. Many plants have evolved to grow in shade, and will not be happy in full sun. This does mean that care must be taken in selecting the right plant for the conditions, but it also means that a shady area should hold less fears.

But what is shade? Shade on the north side of a building, fence or wall is still open to the sky and is less of a problem than the shade cast by a tree, which is almost total. I shall call the former partial shade and the latter full

43

✿ **Full sun**   **partial shade**   **full shade**

shade. More plants will grow in the shade of a wall than under that of a tree.

Dry or damp, acid or alkaline

The type of soil in your garden will also affect your plant selections. As with sun and shade, plants have evolved to grow in different conditions and some have very specific requirements. Most soil is dry, as damp soil is only found in areas with a high water table.

Some common garden plants must have moisture in the soil or they will struggle and eventually die (astilbe is a good example). Others prefer a damp soil, but will cope with some dryness, although they will not achieve the same size. The best approach is to assume that the soil is dry and avoid bog garden plants. Plants which require damp soil and are often planted by mistake in dry soil include, besides astilbes, *Lobelia cardinalis*, some primulas and ferns.

✿ **Rhododendrons are 'edge-of-the-woodland' plants which must have an acid soil.**

The pH (acidity indicator) of the soil can also affect plant selection. A small number must have an acid soil, including rhododendrons, azaleas and most heathers. Without it they will certainly fade away and eventually die. On the other hand, plants which prefer alkaline soil will also grow in acid conditions. If you want to grow an acid-loving plant, and the conditions in the garden are not right, plant it in a container filled with peat-based (ericaceous) compost.

Extreme conditions

Combinations of dry soil and full shade can be a real problem. It is possible to grow plants in these conditions, but they are rarely happy and can look worse than if you simply leave the soil bare.

Under large deciduous trees it is best to plant a succession of spring-flowering bulbs, starting with winter aconites and continuing with snowdrops, crocus, daffodils and other woodland bulbs. These plants have evolved to complete their cycle in the spring before the shady canopy of the tree develops, and are the perfect choice for these conditions. If the bare soil under trees during the rest of the summer is a problem, then design the garden to include a strip of herbaceous perennials in front of the tree, outside its canopy. These plants should all die down in the winter to allow the spring bulbs to be enjoyed, so it is essential that the plants used are all herbaceous – perhaps the only time when I will recommend no structural plants.

No planting should be carried out under evergreens (e.g. yew), as it is doubtful that anything, even bulbs, will survive for very long.

Extreme conditions are not found only under trees. The soil very close to a wall or

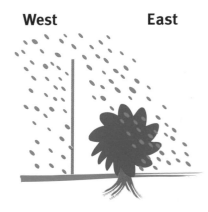

West   **East**

✿ **Where conditions are poor, close to a fence, wall or hedge, select plants with a good spread and plant them in good soil.**

fence is often extremely dry, and eaves and other overhangs from the house can exaggerate the problem. Do not plant within 30cm (12 in) of a wall or fence, and not at all under an overhang. You can plant climbers outside this area and trail them across the ground to reach the structure.

Most of our weather comes from the west, which is where the prevailing wind should be expected. This means that rain tends to come down at an angle from that direction, causing the conditions next to an east-facing wall or fence to be extremely dry. Plants selected for these conditions must be particularly tough. The key to planting here is first to allow as much depth as possible for the border, and then to select plants with a good spread for the back of the border and position their roots as far away from the extreme conditions as possible. This approach could even be taken in front of any overhang.

45

Where to obtain plants and what to order

Availability

If you want to ensure that you have the right plants for your new garden, you must be prepared to place an order with a nursery or garden centre. Plants cannot be bought just by picking them up off the shelf, like groceries – you will be able to find some of them this way, but on the whole you will need to order them. Even then, there will be some plants which, for one reason or another, cannot be found, and you will need to order these plants from a specialist nursery or come up with a viable substitute. To make life easier, be conservative with your selection. Unless you want to make a plant collection, use the same variety of a plant throughout the garden rather than chop and change. For instance, there are a number of different bergenias, but all have large evergreen leathery leaves, pink or white flowers and grow to about the same size. They all look the same from a distance, so, unless you want a white-flowered variety, stick with the same bergenia throughout the garden. Only change to a different variety if there is a good reason – you might want a different colour of leaf or flower, or even a smaller plant. It is often just as easy to obtain twenty plants of one variety as it is to obtain one, but twenty different varieties of the same plant is almost impossible.

What makes a plant difficult to obtain?

The needs of garden centres and public landscaping projects tend to dictate what is grown in any volume, and this is not necessarily compatible with what is best for the private garden. Garden centres want to encourage us to buy their plants and are less interested in what happens after they are sold. They want plants which are happy, and flower well, in small containers – hopefully for a long period. They are also guided by their customers, who expect to be able to buy their favourite and familiar plants. Landscapers, in general, want tough, fast-growing, ground-smothering plants.

Plants which do not fall into these categories can be difficult to obtain, especially in any large numbers, and unfortunately this means that many of the best garden plants are excluded. What are the problems?

Some plants are difficult to propagate, making them uneconomical for anyone other than the most dedicated nurseryman to grow. Most of the problems arise with herbaceous perennials. The normal way of propagating these plants is to cut the root into pieces and plant each piece of root into a new pot, a method which has many benefits, including ensuring that the new plant is true to type and colour. Some plants, however, cannot be propagated in this way. They may need to be grown from seed (like *Geranium psilostemon*), which creates problems in that viable seed must be collected and stored year after year. Any problem with this process and a nursery will have no supplies in a particular season. Some plants simply object to the rough treatment of splitting up. For instance, *Iris foetidissima* 'Variegata', a superb garden plant once established, sulks after it has been divided, so much so that, on many occasions, less than half the new plants survive.

Plants are affected by supply and demand just like any other product. If nobody wants them, nobody is going to grow them. Roses are a classic example. If a rose has not been selling well it will be dropped from the following year's stock. New roses come along each year to replace them, but many varieties can be hard to find, especially the old ones. Sometimes the whole industry is caught out by the popularity of a plant and it vanishes; other times a grower will flood the market with a particular plant, only for an ample supply not to last above a season – the next year it has vanished.

In most cases, the problems are not a reflection on a particular plant's performance in the garden. In fact, if we turn things on their head and look at the plants which are easiest to propagate, we will see that many of them are also the fastest-growing and the most invasive ones.

Plants labelled incorrectly

How can we ensure that the plant we buy is the plant we get? Unless you can personally identify each plant, the best thing is to have the plants checked over by an experienced plantsperson. Every garden centre or nursery will have at least one of these and you should ask him or her to check your order before delivery. Unless a plant is in flower, even the best plantsperson cannot always be certain that it is the correct colour, but if necessary you can get a replacement after it has first flowered.

This solution is not perfect, but it is the best that can be done. If a new plant is not behaving as you expected (it may be larger or smaller), then it may have been labelled incorrectly.

Substitutions

At times it may be necessary to accept a substitute for one or more of the plants in your order. Ask the nurseryman to get in touch and discuss the problem if it arises. A nurseryman's recommendation will normally be based on flower colour, and does not take into account such details as scale. If you do not like the substitute offered, either suggest an alternative of your own or order the correct plant from a nursery listed in *The Plant Finder*.

Rejecting poor plants

Think twice before rejecting a plant because it is in poor condition. Plants tend to look their best at the height of their growing season, which is not necessarily the best time to plant them. It may be that the plant dislikes growing in a container and will be perfectly happy in the open ground.

Some tips about what to look for:

Turn the plant over and remove the pot, carefully holding the top of the soil in the palm of your hand (if the pot will not come free, tap it sharply on the corner of a table or spade handle, and gently squeeze the sides). If the root-ball is a mass of roots, the plant is root-bound – if it is a shrub, conifer or climber reject it. If, however, it is a herbaceous perennial, which will grow fast anyway, it may not be a problem. In fact, perennials in this condition can readily be split into a number of new plants, depending on the size of the container – simply cut the root-ball into pieces with a sharp knife, spade, or even a saw. Evergreens should have healthy foliage and should not have any leaf-bare stems.

In any case, if the plant has been difficult to obtain it may be worth persisting with what you have bought or been sent. You do not need always to start off with an A1 quality plant to achieve a fine specimen in the end, and the fact that so many plants can be improved by very hard pruning suggests that they recover well. Most garden centres and nurseries offer a guarantee; if the offending plant does not recover after planting out you can return it for a replacement.

Plant sizes

Plants come in a variety of pot sizes, the price varying accordingly. The size is usually stamped in the plastic on the underside of the pot. When dealing with a whole garden, considerable savings can be made by ordering smaller plants, but this is not always desirable.

9cm. These are generally the smallest containers used (although some mail order companies use smaller) and are usually square in shape. Herbaceous perennials are best bought in this size in spring or early summer – at any other time of the year buy larger plants, as smaller plants planted in the autumn may not survive their first winter. Shrubs or conifers in this size should be avoided.

1-litre. Treat the same as 9cm containers. Clematis are often offered in this size. These have been micro-propagated and are perfectly all right as long as they are obtained and planted in spring or early summer.

1.5-litre. An odd size. Herbaceous plants are fine in this size, although they may cost a little more than in smaller sizes. Smaller-growing shrubs and conifers like hebes, lavender and santolina, which are fast-growing and establish themselves quickly, will also be fine, although I would be tempted to obtain these only in spring or early summer.

2-litre. Herbaceous perennials, conifers and shrubs tend to come in this size. Again, accept only small-growing conifers and shrubs and expect to pay more for herbaceous plants. Try to avoid larger-growing conifers and shrubs unless this is all that is available. Climbers are normally supplied in 2-litre containers, which are taller and narrower than the normal shape. This is the perfect size for these plants.

3-litre. This is the size to buy conifers and shrubs. Care should be taken in late spring, as this is often the time to move plants into larger containers: if the plant is small it may have just been moved up from a 2-litre pot. Herbaceous plants in this size container will be expensive, but you may be able to chop the root-ball into a number of pieces and perhaps create as many as four plants out of one.

4-litre. Shrubs and conifers in this size will be good-sized specimens and may cost a little more. It is doubtful that you will gain much by paying the extra, but if the plants are a reasonable price snap them up. Herbaceous plants are unlikely to be sold in this size. Roses are normally supplied in 4 litre containers, which are taller and narrower than the normal shape. This is because roses are still grown in open-ground sites and dug up in the winter. The longer containers are designed to accommodate the deep tap-roots.

5-litre upwards. These are regarded as specimen plants and will be sold at a premium. It is useful to include a number of specimen plants in a new garden as they add instant maturity, but make sure that they are truly specimen and not smaller plants in a large pot. Many plants though, are fast-growing, and will quickly create the maturity without the extra expense. Growers will only bother to grow larger plants for which they know there is a demand, so you must be prepared to use whatever is available.

10-litre upwards. This is the best size for trees, and you should not accept them in a smaller size.

Establishing plants

Plants need water, and it is an emotive subject. There is a constant fear among garden owners that their plants are in danger of dying through lack of water. In fact, once established, most plants can survive for long periods without water. The key is to get them well established first. This will involve copious watering every evening for the first few weeks if planted in spring or early summer. The weather conditions will dictate how long to keep this up. In the autumn there is less need for watering, but we seem to get dry spells at any time of the year now, so do not leave the plants to fend for themselves too soon.

Mulches can be applied to help retain moisture, and these are discussed on page 74.

Chapter 5

Planting for effect

One of the great mysteries of the garden is how to create a planting scheme that really works – where every plant enhances and relates to its neighbour and there are few territorial disputes. This is especially problematical for garden designers, who often have little control once the garden has been handed over to the client, but those who are creating their own garden can intervene at any time and deal with difficulties as they occur.

For the busy person it is important not just that a planting scheme is low in maintenance, but that what work needs to be carried out can be done speedily and effectively. This is not as hard as it sounds; the difficulty lies in making it pleasing to the eye. Take a look at the planting around a supermarket car-park; it requires little maintenance, but is, in the main, made up of dull and uninteresting plants planted very close together. The answer is to use the 'car-park' plants as the backbone to a scheme and incorporate the more colourful and interesting ones in and around them.

Although it is best to start with a plan, once planted it will invariably need modifying as it develops. Many plants are unpredictable – sometimes a particular plant will grow much faster and larger than expected, while another will not perform at all. This uncertainty can be a problem if we remain rigid in our approach, but until we know exactly how a particular plant is going to behave in our garden, we must stick with the information that is readily available in gardening books, encyclopaedias and nursery catalogues. Many of these will give details of what size a plant is expected to reach after a certain period, usually five, ten or fifteen years, and these should be our guide at the outset. For instance, if you want your garden to be at its best after ten years, allow each plant the space indicated in the literature. Gardening books can be inconsistent, so stick with one, where possible, for all your plant sizes, or look at detailed nursery catalogues, which I have found to be more reliable and up to date. It will take at least a year before a true evaluation can be made of any problems with a plant, so try not to make hasty decisions.

Another word about plant growth: you cannot expect the plants in your garden to reach a certain size and then stop. This means that at some time in the future some drastic changes will be required, perhaps even a total re-design. When this occurs will depend upon how long you have allowed for the garden to reach its ultimate size. Problems will occur approximately five to ten years after your garden has reached its chosen height.

We have talked a lot about plant sizes, but how do you decide which plants will make good companions? The surefire way is to concentrate initially on plant and leaf shape, incorporating as many different ones into a scheme as possible. Flower colour can be fleeting, perhaps lasting only a few weeks, whereas the different shapes, tones and textures of green can be there for much longer, in some cases all the year round.

✿ **An eye-catching display like this one in a Chelsea Flower Show garden, designed by David Stevens, does not happen by accident. There is little colour; the overall effect is created by the careful selection of plant and leaf shapes.**

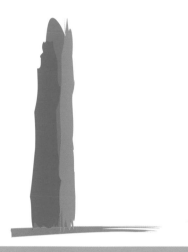

✿ **Fastigiate shape.**

✿ *Hebe rakaiensis* **forms a solid round ball shape without the need for clipping. It is also evergreen.**

✿ *Verbascum*, **or** *mullein*, **has fine fastigiate flowers in midsummer. This variety is** *Verbascum chaixii* **'Album'.**

✿ **'Ball' and fastigiate shapes.**

Plant shapes

Upright or fastigiate

The contrast between a bun shape and that of a column or pillar is the most striking in any arrangement. The difficulty is finding plants that grow in the latter fashion. Conifers supply the lion's share, but they can be a problem – most conifers dislike other plants growing too close because it causes their foliage to die back, in most cases never to return. Some herbaceous perennials, delphiniums for example, have upright flower spikes which are useful but are, of course, seasonal. Plants with the desired shape include *Juniperus scopulorum* 'Skyrocket', delphiniums, lupins, *Taxus baccata* 'Fastigiata' and *digitalis* (foxgloves).

Ball or bun shape

This is a fairly staid shape, and a garden can appear overly formal if too many are used. It is a shape, however, which is critical to the balance within a design. Plants like *Hebe rakaiensis*, *H. toparia*, *Choisya ternata*, *Buxus sempervirens* (which can be clipped into

✿ The wedding-cake tree, *Cornus controversa* **'Variegata'**, is a delightful contribution to a planting scheme, although it can be very slow-growing.

✿ **'Ball', fastigiate and horizontal shapes.**

✿ **Ball, fastigiate, horizontal and weeping shapes.**

✿ A good example of a plant that will always 'weep' effectively in the garden is *Cedrus deodora* **'Golden Horizon'**.

53

✿ *Phormium tenax* **'Purpureum' is a fine spiky-leafed plant for the larger arrangement. There are smaller phormiums, but they may not be as hardy.**

✿ **Ball, fastigiate, horizontal, weeping and spiky shapes.**

almost any shape) and *Thuja orientalis* 'Aurea Nana' all provide this shape.

Horizontal

This flat shape is usually added by using ground-hugging perennials or shrubs, but some plants, like *Viburnum plicatum* 'Mariesii' and *Cornus controversa* 'Variegata' (the wedding-cake tree), have tiered branches growing in layers. Care should be taken when selecting horizontally growing plants as many can be invasive and will bully their neighbours. Try *Juniperus horizontalis*, *Hebe* 'Carl Teschner' or *Acaena microphylla*.

Weeping

This shape adds drama and impact. Everyone thinks of the weeping willow, which, while it will create the desired effect on a grand scale, is too large for the average garden. Many smaller plants have a weeping habit and others give the impression of weeping where their branches turn over at the tips. Plants like *Genista lydia* (a variety of broom) and

Fuchsia 'Mrs Popple' give the desired effect, and there is also a small weeping willow called *Salix caprea* 'Pendula' (Kilmarnock willow), although I find this difficult to use in a mixed planting scheme. Weeping standard roses can be useful; try *Rosa* 'Nozomi' or *R.* 'Suma' (make sure you select standard roses – the ordinary shrub versions of these plants are rampant landscapers).

Spiky

This is the most dramatic shape of all, and perhaps the most important. Unlike other plant shapes, this description tends to refer to the leaves rather than the overall plant. Sometimes I am asked to look at a border which is full of colour but lacking in interest; the owner is aware of the problem, but cannot pinpoint it. It is usually because the border lacks this shape, and my solution is simple – add small groups of *Iris germanica*, or another spiky-leafed plant, intermittently throughout the bed. The correction is instant and notable.

❀ *Bergenia ciliata* **is unusual in that it is deciduous, whereas most of this genus are evergreen.**

❀ **Ball, fastigiate, horizontal, weeping, spiky and large-leafed shapes.**

You will notice that I recommend planting the irises in small groups. This is important. Large groups of this shape can result in a loss of impact and can totally change the character of the planting; it is no accident that Disneyland plant lots of grasses, yuccas and other spiky plants in their 'Frontierland' to give the effect of a hot dry climate. Plants to use include: *Yucca gloriosa*, *Iris foetidissima* 'Variegata', kniphofias (red hot pokers), grasses and phormiums

Large round-leafed

The large round leaves of many herbaceous perennials and some shrubs have a tremendous capacity for bringing out the best in the plants around them. Again, these plants have more impact in small groups. They include bergenias, hostas, brunneras and catalpa.

'Woofly'

This final category is used to describe plants with fine feathery, textured or interesting foliage which cannot be categorized under one of the above headings. In large groups they can be untidy, but planted next to a formal ball or fastigiate shape they can complete a scheme. Plants that fit into this group include *Salvia officinalis* (sage), *Acer palmatum* 'Dissectum' (Japanese cut-leafed maple) and *Alchemilla mollis* (lady's mantle).

Building up a plan

Split the garden up into areas and decide on a main flowering season for each one. This is a much better approach than trying to make the whole garden look good at every season of the year – each area will reach a crescendo of concentrated colour at its allotted time rather than the colour being dotted around the whole garden. Many plants will overlap flowering seasons, so there will be some colour in areas outside their season.

Each flowering season should be for a period of two or three months. For instance April/May, June/July, August/September, October/November/December,

✿ **'Woofly' plants:** *Acer palmatum* **'Dissectum', sage and hellebores.**

✿ **Ball, fastigiate, horizontal, weeping, spiky, large-leafed and woofly shapes.**

✿ **A completed scheme should include a range of plant and leaf shapes in order to be a success.**

✿ **The main border at Coton Manor in Northamptonshire is the highlight of the garden in mid-summer. It is a traditional herbaceous border and is much admired by thousands of summer visitors.**

January/February/March. (Winter-flowering is much sparser – it may be better to treat the winter months as secondary displays to the summer ones.)

Try to place winter and spring flowers close to the house where they can be best enjoyed – there is no point in hiding them away in a position where they will not be seen.

In small gardens it may not be possible to have the flowering in seasonal blocks. In this instance look for plants with a long flowering season.

The structure

Many of us want our gardens to be one large herbaceous border, overflowing with bright colourful picture-postcard plants, like those cottage gardens from a previous era. The problem with this is that few of the plants used in such a scheme have any structure and many are at their best for perhaps only two months of the year, completely vanishing below the ground during the winter. This is fine if your garden is large enough, because then you can have a border for each month of the year, but if, like the majority of garden owners, your space is limited, each plant must be able to earn its place.

The key to a successful all-year-round planting scheme is to ensure that structural plants are heavily represented, by which I mean plants with a solid presence during the winter. Normally evergreen, they form a framework on which the colours can be built up and the changing seasons marked, in the safe knowledge that the whole

✿ **In winter, however, the majority of the plants in this border hibernate for the duration. This is fine at Coton, where the garden is closed during the winter, as it allows essential maintenance and upgrading. In the private garden, in use all the year round, this lack of structure can be a real problem.**

scheme is built on a secure footing. Try to ensure a ratio of one third evergreen to two-thirds deciduous in a normal area, but reverse this for a front garden or somewhere used extensively during the winter months, when more structure will be required.

I have referred to evergreens when talking about structural plants, but many deciduous plants have a winter presence. Winter-flowering shrubs and trees are also very useful for brightening up the garden during a period when we all need a psychological lift.

One danger with structural plants, though, is in using too many. Although they can be very low-maintenance, over-use can remove much of the character from the garden, leaving it flat and lifeless with little to mark the changing seasons.

The 'flowering season' of a particular area will be determined by the deciduous shrubs and perennial 'fill-in' plants. Although evergreens have a flowering season, it is more important to use them to create balance and structure throughout the whole garden. To this end do not be afraid to use the same plant over and over again.

✿ **A well designed border will look good all year round. This border benefits from a fine summer display including Rosa 'Golden Wings', Geranium 'Johnson's Blue' and Alchemilla mollis.**

✿ **In winter, structural plants like Mahonia japonica, Cornus alba, bergenias and Juniperus 'Skyrocket' take over ensuring that there is all year round interest.**

Chapter 6

Creating the Garden

Any form of labour-intensive work has its problems, and landscaping has more than its fair share. If the construction has not been carried out to a sufficiently high standard, problems are being stored up for the future – problems which in extreme cases can destroy a garden.

When employing a contractor I would always employ a qualified landscape gardener rather than a builder. A garden is very different from a building – it is exposed to the elements more, and structures must be able to cope with the rigours of the British climate. Gardens should be relaxed, unhurried places, where it is less important to find the shortest route between two points than it is in a building. There should be a thought process

at work in the garden which most builders are not attuned to, whereas a good landscape gardener will be aware of the many problems and will know how to cope with them.

In this chapter we shall look at the critical areas of garden construction – areas where there is an optimum way of doing things or where I have encountered problems. This is not intended to be a training manual, but a guide to problem areas of construction and what to look out for.

Paving material

Bricks vs. Pavers

Basically, a brick is designed for use in walls and a paver, as the name suggests, is used for paving. The key thing, as far as paving is concerned, is that they are different shapes. A typical brick is 22 x 7 x 10cm (8.5 x 2.5 x 4in), whereas a paver is 20 x 10 x 5cm (8 x 4 x 2in) (the last measurement, or thickness, can vary).

Each will have one or two faces which are intended to face outwards and be seen. These will differ depending upon whether it is a brick or a paver: bricks have the facing on one of the long edges and one of the end edges, whereas pavers are designed to be laid flat, so the face is one of the large flat sides. Sometimes, exposing the wrong face can spoil the look of a design.

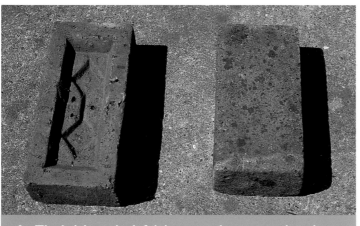

✿ **The brick on the left is longer and narrower than the paver on the right. The frogging is designed to ensure a good amount of cement between one brick and the next in a wall. Some bricks have holes running through the whole structure instead of frogging, which can cause a problem when they are laid flat. The shape of the paver means that it is twice as long as it is wide, making it the perfect choice for patterns like basketweave and herringbone.**

✿ **Bricks can make a fine path when laid frog side down. Here, some of the bricks used are not frost-resistant and have suffered winter damage, but in this instance it has added to the character of the scene.**

the odd failure. Before making a decision, contact your local builder's yard and ask for details of the bricks he holds in stock, and which ones are frost-resistant.

Whatever course you take, frost-resistant or otherwise, it is always a good idea to obtain more than you require for the job. The spare ones can be stored away somewhere in the garden for use later, should any replacements be required. They will weather at the same rate as those in the garden, ensuring a good colour match should some later surgery be required.

Another problem with brick is that for most garden projects the number required is comparatively low. With small orders you will be charged haulage by the manufacturer, often making the project unviable. One answer is to select your brick from whatever the local builder's yard already holds in stock. Alternatively you could search out a brick factor, someone who acts as the middle man between a builder and the brick manufacturer. Both these courses can be very restrictive and, if nothing is suitable, you will either have to look further afield, pay the haulage, or arrange to collect your bricks from the manufacturer yourself.

Pavers

Pavers can be split into two types: concrete and clay. The latter are made from the same material as bricks, although you can assume that they are hard enough to use in paving. Those made from concrete are extremely hard, so there is no fear of them breaking up in the frost.

From the aesthetic point of view, the colour of concrete pavers has to be added using dyes, whereas the colour of clay pavers is natural. Concrete pavers can therefore look

Bricks

In the right setting there is nothing like a brick path to enhance a garden. The problem is that most bricks are not hard enough to use in paving and their surface will tend to break up in the frost. This may of course give the desired effect, but must be borne in mind when you are installing a path. If you want the garden to be solid and last for years, you must select a brick which is at least frost-resistant, and even then you may experience

✿ **The concrete pavers used in this mowing strip have faded badly and look extremely uncomfortable next to the mellow clay bricks of the wall. It is also clear that the mowing strip has been constructed incorrectly – nobody explained what a mowing strip was to the builder.**

a little artificial and often the red colours fade to pink with age, whereas clay pavers mellow and improve over the same time period.

The use of bricks and pavers

Perhaps the most common use for pavers is in the front driveway, a practice that is not always successful. The drive is usually the first impression anyone has of the garden and house and for this reason it must be welcoming. Sadly, most drives are installed with one thing in mind: to provide as much parking space as possible, with unhindered access to the garage. This often creates a sea of hard red paving, spoiling the look of both house and garden. With some thought, however, we can cater quite successfully for the motor car and produce a pleasing, welcoming garden.

The key thing to remember is that there are always spaces where the motor car cannot reach or perhaps does not need to go. It is in these areas that plants can be grown which will grow over the edge of the pavers and thereby soften it. If you have a requirement for an occasional parking space or even an 'in and out' turning area, consider using contrasting materials to give the impression that this extra space is part of the garden, not the driveway. In certain circumstances this additional space can double as an extension to the patio or sitting area. It can be effective to use pea shingle with stepping stones and the odd ground-hugging alpine, bearing in mind that these plants must be away from the areas where tyres may pass.

As you might imagine from reading the above, it is imperative that a plan is drawn to scale on paper (1 cm to 1 m (1 to 100) is a good size to choose). Cut out two or three rectangles of paper, to scale, to represent cars (4.5 x 1.8 m is a size which should cover most cars), and use these to work out the extent of the paved area you need. Do not forget that car doors have to open and driver and passengers must have room to alight. Look for spaces, usually close to the building, where plants can be used instead of paving. If you want to plant ground-hugging alpines in a disguised turning area, work out spots safe from any car tyres; these may well be under the centre of the car's chassis.

There is always a danger that accidents will happen when manoeuvring a car, and

✿ **The paved area to the right of the front door can be used for the cars to turn. It is attractive and practical.**

✿ Mixing pavers with paving slabs can be effective in breaking up the space as well as drawing the house and other structures into the garden. The use of strong lines and pavers in this Chelsea Flower Show garden contributed to the designer, David Stevens, winning a Gold Medal.

plants become crushed as a result. It is therefore important to mark the edge of a bed with something that will indicate to the driver that he is about to leave the confines of the driveway. There are specially designed edging blocks available, which, if sufficiently high, will deter a driver, or ordinary pavers could be set on their ends, although this can look very untidy. Corners of beds can be a problem, especially on the edge of turning areas; a good way to deal with these is to install cobblestones embedded in concrete.

The choice of colour for a driveway is also critical to the final result. Red concrete pavers are the most common choice, but are often selected without any thought. Pavers now come in a range of colours, many of which might be more pleasing to the eye than red. As was discussed in Chapter 3, the house is the largest feature in the garden and needs careful treatment to integrate it, if the garden is to be a success. This is also true of the front garden, and copying elements from the house in the driveway is one way of creating a link. Using a paver to match the colour of the house is a good method, but, as most houses are constructed from red brick, that brings us back to the ubiquitous sea of red which is the basis of so many problems. I favour using a neutral-coloured paver over most of the area but with small patterns picking up colours from the house. The colour of the brickwork has already been discussed, but there are often browns and dark greys in the woodwork and roof which could be picked up.

We have so far concentrated on concrete pavers, as these are the most common and also the cheapest; however, as I have mentioned, the reds can have a rather unnatural colour. If the money will stretch to it, use clay pavers, as these will

'Hurried' patterns

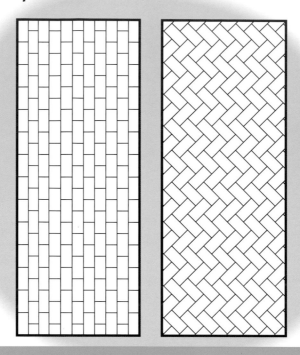

'Away' stretcher bond

'Away' herringbone

weather better and be closer in colour to that of the house.

Because pavers are used so much for driveways, it can be difficult to envisage their use elsewhere in the garden. I certainly feel that a patio made from pavers is somehow coarse and uninviting, but they can be used in small areas. Pavers can be used as an edging to the lawn, or mowing strip, although a brick on edge has a better look. Mowing strips are discussed in more detail on page 34.

Pavers are also very useful for paths. Ideally use clay and try to pick up the colour of a brick used in the house, but if the finance does not stretch to it, use concrete, carefully selecting the style and colour. When laying pavers in paths the choice of pattern can affect the character of the structure. If the pattern chosen has the main lines running along the length of the path, away from the user, the path will appear hurried and purposeful; if the

pattern runs across the path, from left to right, it will be relaxed and unhurried. Your choice of pattern should therefore depend on the use that the path is to be put to.

Gardens should be relaxed places, so why would anyone want to introduce a 'hurried' pattern? The reason is that there are times when it is useful to guide visitors in a particular direction, perhaps when the property has two entrances and it can be difficult for a visitor to determine which one is the main one. In this instance, a 'hurried' path will often show the way.

See also page 32.

Paving slabs

Natural stone

In previous generations, the term 'slabs' when referring to the house or garden meant pieces of hard natural stone cut thin enough to be

'Relaxed' patterns

| 'Across' stretcher bond | Basketweave | 'Across' herringbone |

used on the ground. As materials didn't travel far, these had to come from the local area, so if the local stone was not hard enough, or was too hard to cut, as in the case of granite, people tended to turn to other materials and the culture of using slabs never developed. As transport improved, the use of slabs became more widespread, the two most commonly used being Yorkstone (a hard sandstone from Yorkshire) and Portland (a hard limestone from Dorset). In fact Yorkstone has become the archetypal slab, with most artificial versions being moulded to simulate it.

Yorkstone is still the best paving slab and seems to fit with most styles of house or garden. It is expensive, however, and is treated as a commodity, meaning that the price goes up and down with the market. Slabs come in two thicknesses: up to 2 inches (most come from Yorkshire, where imperial measurements still rule) and larger

than 2 inches. The thicker is actually the cheaper of the two because it is more difficult to handle, but it can be laid with virtually no foundation so long as enough hands are available to manoeuvre it.

One word of warning: only buy Yorkstone from a reliable source. Some has been lifted from the floor of old factories and may have bolt-holes in it and be impregnated with oil – something you may not be able to see, but which will come to the surface with wear. New Yorkstone is available fresh from the quarry if you are concerned about the source.

Portland stone is still available and can be used in paving, but it tends to cost more than Yorkstone. There are some other local stones that could be used, but make sure that they are hard enough for paving. Just as with bricks, if the stone is soft, water will seep in and the paving will crumble in the frost – a process that can happen quite quickly.

✿ **The genuine Yorkstone on the left is almost indistinguishable from the lookalike version on the right.**

Artificial stone

There have been artificial paving slabs around for as long as I can remember – all made of concrete and most with a riven surface to simulate Yorkstone. It is only very recently that these lookalikes have actually started to look like the real thing. In fact, at times it can be difficult to tell which is the copy.

Although in most cases a Yorkstone lookalike would be the best choice, there are times when a different surface is more appropriate. For instance, around a swimming pool, where it is essential to have a non-slip surface, a plainer slab with a rougher surface would be a better choice. There are

also slabs made to simulate limestone paving taken from a watermill, and this might be appropriate in some settings.

Pea shingle

This hard surface has been used in gardens almost as long as the concept of gardening has existed. Not only is it the cheapest hard surface, but it is also the one that is most pleasing to the eye. Unlike most other paving materials it is unpretentious, complementing plants and forming a background against which they can best be displayed. Regardless of the style of garden – whether it is Georgian, Victorian, Edwardian or twentieth-century, country, cottage or town – the use of pea shingle in one form or another is always right.

Unfortunately, this material has been tainted in recent years. Not because of its look, but because of the shoddy way it is too often laid, leading to a deep layer of heavy-duty stones which is not only uncomfortable to walk through but can also damage shoes and cause pushchairs, wheelbarrows and even cars to stick like glue. The culprit is a comparatively new material called 'type 1' or MOT, which is basically a mixture of granite chips and dust.

✿ **Granite chips break away from the lower layer of MOT or 'type 1' and float to the surface of the gravel, spoiling the effect.**

The contractor will consolidate this with a vibrating plate and then cover it with a layer of gravel; because of the nature of the MOT, this layer must be fairly thick. There is no binding agent in the MOT so, after a period of time, pieces of granite break loose and 'float' to the surface of the gravel, adding to the mess. Sometimes they will use a finer MOT called 'type 2' which gives a slightly better result, but it still lacks a binding agent and requires an overly thick layer of gravel.

Until the advent of MOT, gravel paths had been laid in the same way for many years. The sub-base was made up of a substance called hoggin, which is a mixture of clay, sand and shingle, and it was available in three different grades, from fine through to rough. This was rolled, then watered to soften the surface and rolled again, until a sound hoggin path was made. After this the surface was watered again and a layer of small grade pea shingle was rolled into the surface. The finished path was then sprinkled with some loose pea shingle. Once in use, the pea shingle slowly worked its way down into the hoggin, making the path harder and stronger. This method works because of the clay content in the hoggin, which acts as a binding agent, combining with the pea shingle to make a solid path. MOT cannot do this and the layers remain loose and separate.

True hoggin (take care, as some people now use this term for MOT) can be difficult to find, and when you do find it, it tends to be very rough, with lots of large lumps embedded in it. A good source would be a gravel pit, as hoggin is often a by-product. But what if hoggin simply cannot be found? The key to it is clay. If you have a clay soil, prepare that just as you would hoggin,

69

✿ **Hoggin alone has been used to great effect in the paths at Hidcote, Gloucestershire.**

perhaps even going deeper and bringing up some of the heavier subsoil.

Because of the problem with weeds, some people recommend laying a piece of geotextile material under the gravel. This acts a barrier through which the weeds cannot grow. The problem is the same one as that created by the MOT: there is no interface between the pea shingle and the sub-layer. The pea shingle, or gravel, is loose and must be laid in a deep layer to be effective.

How, therefore, do we deal with the weeds? First, and this should be done whatever method is used, you must dispose of all the weeds in the area of the path. Some of the roots will persist, and these could force their way through to the surface. The best solution is to treat the area with a systemic weedkiller which will destroy the roots as well (see page 75). Once the perennial weeds have been dealt with, as long as the hoggin, or clay soil, has been well consolidated, few weeds will be able to establish themselves in or just

✿ **This path has been created on compacted clay soil; it is comfortable and easy to walk on.**

71

✿ **Decking has been used to great effect by Richard Key in this garden at the Chelsea Flower Show.**

below the surface of the pea shingle. Those that appear will be weak and can easily be dealt with by hand, or with further applications of weedkiller. The small nuisance value of dealing with one or two small weeds is better than the alternative. See Chapter 7 for more details of weed eradication.

In some situations, having a loose material like pea shingle is not an option, for instance on a slope where it will migrate to the bottom, creating a small pile. A viable alternative would be sealed gravel, which is pea shingle rolled into wet tarmacadam or exposed aggregate (see 'concrete'). Tarmac on

its own is a poor choice for a garden – nothing could look less natural and be more difficult to combine with ornamental plants.

Concrete

A well constructed concrete path can last for many years, but in fact most of them crack and break up after just a few. The look tends not to be very attractive, but can be improved by washing off the top layer of cement while it is still wet, thereby exposing the aggregate, an effect close to that of pea shingle or gravel. This is referred to as exposed aggregate.

into an almost infinite number of shapes, meaning that paving material which would normally not be hardy enough for the British climate can be used, albeit in a simulated form. This is particularly useful outside a conservatory or kitchen, where it might be desirable to continue the paving into the garden.

The problem is that it is impossible to make changes after it is laid and can be expensive; an important consideration if you are unsure of how the garden will develop.

Decking

As with 'pressed' concrete, wooden decking is usually installed in the mistaken belief that it is a cheaper alternative. In fact, if the right wood is used and it is properly installed, it can cost more. The wood used must be designed for use in decking – do not use ordinary wood. It will be pressure-treated (see note below) and impregnated with a fungicide. Wood is notorious for being slippery when wet, and this is usually caused by fungal build-up, which the fungicide is designed to deal with.

Note on pressure-treating: the preserving chemical is forced into the wood using high-pressure equipment, but this can only be fully effective if the chemical reaches right into the centre of the wood. To do this the wood must be totally dry before the procedure begins – a function which is carried out in a special drying kiln. A lot of wood is pressure-treated without this drying step, resulting in a product which has a shorter life than would otherwise be the case. The best way to check if wood has been pressure-treated properly is to inspect the guarantee – anything twenty years or over should be fine.

Concrete can expand and contract, so ensure that expansion joints are built in.

'Pressed' concrete

In recent years this style of paving has been imported from America. It involves dyeing the concrete and pressing a pattern into the surface before the cement dries. I say concrete, but the formula used means that it is much more durable than ordinary concrete. I am not aware of any structural problems, although the colour can appear a little unnatural.

Its advantage is that it can be pressed

Chapter 7

Ground Preparation

As I have said earlier in this book, the key to a successful, easily maintained garden is forward planning and preparation. Nowhere is this more important than with the soil. Pernicious weeds must be dealt with and the soil well fed before any planting is carried out.

Weeds

Before planting an area of ground, you must first ensure that it is clear of weeds. Low-maintenance planting will become a nightmare if it becomes infested with weeds, so the importance of this preparation cannot be underestimated. If there is a serious problem it is best to wait until it has been dealt with, even if that means leaving any planting until the following season.

'A weed is a plant growing in the wrong place' is an over-used phrase but one which best describes the problem. Most weeds are highly successful, invasive and colonizing wild plants, but some cultivated garden plants can also become a serious nuisance. A look at the section on plants to avoid (see page 150) will give plenty of warnings.

If you have just taken over a garden it is useful to decide whether or not weeds are going to be a serious problem. If the garden has been well tended for a number of years, the chances are that what weeds there are can be dealt with fairly easily. If the garden has been neglected, or the land has been uncultivated (perhaps a new house on an old piece of farmland), it will be full of weed seeds just waiting for just this opportunity to arise. The latter could be an unseen but serious problem, so be prepared.

As with all plants, weeds can be pigeon-holed as perennials, annuals or even biennials. The latter two grow from dormant seeds which may have been lying in the ground for

years waiting for the right growing conditions (usually sunlight and water), before bursting forth. The best way of dealing with them is to deny them these conditions and, as we need water so that our other plants can grow, we must contrive a way of keeping the weed seeds in the dark, away from any light. This is best done by mulching the soil. A mulch is material, either organic or inorganic, laid across the top of the soil, insulating it from the elements but also allowing the ornamental perennial plants to grow through. It can be made of anything from old carpet to polythene, from grass cuttings to composted bark – the key is to keep the ground in the dark and stop the weed seeds from germinating. The final choice should be

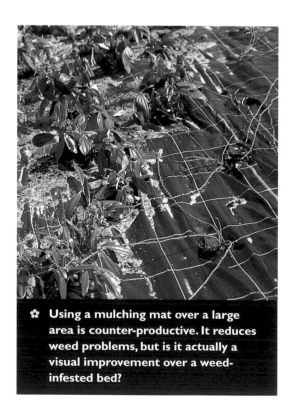

✿ **Using a mulching mat over a large area is counter-productive. It reduces weed problems, but is it actually a visual improvement over a weed-infested bed?**

✿ **A mulching mat is certainly not a total solution, and perennial weeds must still be dealt with before it is applied. Bindweed, and many other perennial weeds, cannot be killed by it.**

made on the basis of looks and not expedience.

Man-made mulching material has become very popular in recent years, but in itself is not attractive and needs to be disguised. This is usually done with composted forest bark or pea shingle, and when you want to plant you cut a cross to accommodate the roots. I find this matting, over a large area, very unsatisfactory: first there is no contact between the soil and the disguising material, which is often spread around by animals or the wind, exposing the matting beneath; second, the plants are restricted so that they cannot spread to provide the desired ground-covering. Having said all this, I do find it useful under hedges or around newly planted trees to conserve water. Soil can be used in these situations to disguise it.

The best solution is to apply a natural-coloured organic material as a mulch: either composted bark or coir, good compost or manure. The key thing is that it must look good and provide a canvas on which the planting can be displayed. This organic material will rot down in time but can be replenished, in the case of compost or manure, annually, or when the ground-cover effect has gone. I have found that low-maintenance planting takes about three years to start to take effect and it is at this time that forest bark ceases to be effective. So for an easy life use forest bark or coir. These can be expensive, however, which is where compost and manure win. As with many things in the garden, there is a trade-off

between cost and labour: the latter is cheaper but you need to obtain and spread it each spring, whereas the former is expensive initially, saving money in the long run.

In order to ensure that annual and biennial weed seeds are kept in the dark, it is critical that any organic matter laid on the surface is 5cm (2in) deep. Any less than this and the mulch will be ineffective. If cost is a consideration, then mulch a smaller area to the required depth rather than spreading a smaller amount across the whole garden.

With perennial weeds mulching has little effect, although it will deter their seeds from germinating and make them easier to spot. They will even find ways through or round a mulching mat. We must therefore kill weeds first. Most can be dug out carefully by hand, or with a suitable tool, extracting as much of the root as possible. Some, however, have persistent and spreading roots, the tiniest piece of which will grow a new plant, and these are best dealt with using a weedkiller. There is a lot of prejudice against the use of weedkillers in the garden, and

75

✿ *Cedrus deodora* 'Golden Horizon' is the perfect choice for the edge of a pool, where the weeping branches can hang over the water.

quite rightly so, but with plants like bindweed, whose roots have been found 30 metres down in coalmines, there is little choice. Only use the quantity of weedkiller necessary for the job and only on the weeds that cannot be dealt with in any other way. The following weeds are the only ones which need treating in this way: the tiniest piece of root from these weeds will regrow a new plant, so do not allow a rotavator near the area as this will simply multiply the problem.

Bindweed (both hedge and field): A perennial climbing plant whose foliage does not appear above the ground until quite late in the growing season.

Ground elder: A carpeting perennial with summer flowers similar to that of ordinary elder.

Couch grass: A running grass.

There are basically two types of weedkiller: contact and systemic. Contact weedkillers simply burn off the top of the plant, which then happily regrows from the root – a waste of time and money unless you persist in its use, applying it on a regular basis. A weed will eventually die if it continually loses its foliage as soon as it appears.

Systemic weedkillers work by soaking into the whole plant and destroying it from the inside out. These are the ones to use. The chemical currently in use for this job is glyphosate, which is present in a number of different brands of weedkiller. If the label does not say that it contains this chemical then it will not. Glyphosate works on growing tissue and is less effective later in the season when the plants are concentrating on producing seed and root growth, so the best time to use it is earlier when the plant's effort is in producing top growth. I am also a little concerned about the temperature at which weedkillers are effective; they seem to work better in warmer weather.

Ideally, start your campaign in early to mid-May, depending upon the temperature, and apply the

✿ **Bindweed can turn a low-maintenance planting scheme into a nightmare.**

✿ **Field horsetail, sometimes called mare's tail.**

a nearby plant for six days, until the weedkiller has soaked in, then removed and the weed foliage cut off at ground level.

You will probably need to apply the weed-killer more than once before the job is done, so, once each application has done its work, water the area to encourage re-growth. Once a lush growth has been achieved, strike again.

With a serious infestation of the difficult weeds mentioned earlier, where the roots have got into a bed of ornamental plants, drastic action will be needed. Because the tiniest piece of root will regrow into a new weed, removing the ornamental plants, dealing with the weeds and then returning them will simply bring the problem back. The only answer is to kill all the herbaceous plants alongside the weeds and retain just the larger shrubs. Hopefully, the weeds close to the shrubs can be dealt with separately. It is drastic, I know, but remember, we are aiming to create an easily maintainable garden and this will involve some sacrifices.

Sometimes the weeds persist in a neighbour's garden, from where they will invade your weed-free patch. Unless you can hop over the fence and deal with the problem over there, all your hard work could be for nothing. The only solution is to design the garden to allow a strip of ungardened ground, 30–45cm (12–18in) wide, close to the offending boundary. Regular patrols of this

weedkiller on a dry evening to give the chemical all night to soak in. It takes about two weeks to work, but will have permeated the plant's system after six days. Where the problem is not great, the weedkiller can be painted on to the leaves by mixing it with a strong solution of washing-up liquid. It is important that none of the solution makes contact with any garden plants which are to be kept – any splashes can be washed off with plain water, or the affected leaves removed by hand (wear gloves). With climbing weeds like bindweed, which could wave around in the wind depositing weedkiller far and wide, put some solution into a milk bottle or jar, unravel a length of the weed and stuff it into the receptacle. This can then be hidden under area should be made and any sorties from next door rapidly dealt with – keep a paint-on solution of systemic weedkiller handy, as this way you can counterattack the weeds beyond the fence.

There is one very serious weed that has not been mentioned: field horsetail (sometimes known as mare's tail, but this is a misnomer). The Christmas-tree-like growths are very distinctive and tend to prefer damp soil. Glyphosate has a limited effect and will only, at best, weaken the plants. One saving grace is that it tends to be a localised problem and is rarely seen all over a garden. Careful digging with a border fork, removing as much of the root system as possible, will reduce the problem to a manageable level. After this, pull up any 'Christmas trees' that appear – eventually the weed will be weakened so much that it will die out.

Improving the soil

Once the weeds have been dealt with we must turn our attention to the soil. The success, or otherwise, of the project could depend upon this critical stage, so it must not be skimped. The problem for most people is that this work is invisible to them; it can cost a lot of money and take a fair bit of work, at the end of which there is very little to show for it. The rewards for this work will eventually manifest themselves, but not for a year or two.

Before the plants go in, the soil is freely accessible, perhaps for the last time in many years, and we must take full advantage of this, digging in as much soil-improving material as possible. There are many different soil types and we could look at the best way to prepare each type, but that can become unnecessarily complex. We will pigeonhole the soil as either

a sandy loam, a clay loam or an acid soil (the latter could be either sandy or clay).

Sandy soil

A sandy soil consists of quite large particles which do not readily stick together; it is very open, dries out quickly and nutrients are quickly washed away. It is a very difficult soil to deal with, requiring copious amounts of manure or compost to bulk it out and hold the nutrients and moisture. These should be applied annually in the spring.

Clay loam

A clay loam consists of tiny particles which readily cling together; it can be stodgy when wet and crack like poor cement when dry. Although difficult to work, it is generally very fertile, holding on to its nutrients, and most plants will thrive in it. Incorporating sand, or something similar, will lighten it and make it easier to work. Manure and peat or its alternatives will help to condition it. Finally, keep off it as much as possible, as treading on the soil causes compaction and can make it rock-hard.

Most soils have a degree of both elements, sand and clay, within them, and you must decide which element your soil has most of. You can find this out by taking a lump and rolling it around in your hand (add water if the sample is too dry) – the more it sticks together, the more the clay content. If in doubt talk to neighbours; if the locality has a problem soil they will have many stories to tell.

Acid soil

Some plants must have an acid soil and will die without it, so it is important to decide whether your soil is acid or alkaline. This can be defined by using a kit from the garden centre, which is easy to use. The term pH is used to define acidity; 7.0 is neutral, anything higher than this is alkaline and lower is acid. For sandy or clay soils treat the soil as defined previously, but do not use mushroom compost on acid or neutral soil as this will increase the pH, possibly turning it alkaline.

Use one or more of the following to improve the soil.

Well-rotted manure or compost

This is a good soil-enricher, fertilizer and bulking agent. Every type of soil should have this incorporated – annually for sandy soils. It must be well rotted and have a sweet smell – it can take at least twelve months to get to this stage. Fresh manure will burn the plants and their roots and take nitrogen from the soil as it breaks down, so should be avoided. Manure can also be used as a mulch.

Obtaining manure can sometimes be a problem, but larger builders' merchants should be able to supply some. Alternatively look for advertisements in the local paper. There is usually plenty about, the problem being transportation. There are some addresses on page 157 which may help. Used mushroom compost is readily available and a good choice in most cases (see 'Acid Soil').

Sand

Use this to lighten clay soils. Any sand should do the job, but avoid builders' soft sand as it can be dirty and greasy. Sharp sand is the best, but it can be expensive; I usually specify washed river sand, which is normally used for laying pavers and is a cheaper alternative.

Peat or a peat alternative

I do not specify the use of peat because of the damage its removal is doing to the environment, however it has to be said that there is still nothing to match it as a soil conditioner. Alternatives have been created using coir and compost, but quite frankly these are less effective.

In conclusion

With a sandy soil lay a 5cm (2in) layer of well-rotted manure or compost (mixed 50/50 with peat if required) over the soil and then dig it in using either a spade or a rotavator. Apply this annually, laid across the soil as a mulch and/or lightly forked into the surface.

With a clay soil mix well-rotted manure with sand in equal parts and lay a 5cm (2in) layer across the soil before digging or rotavating it in. Because of the nature of clay soil, it will not be necessary to apply the mixture in a mulch every year, but perhaps every three or four.

Do not go down lower than a spade's depth, as this may bring undesirable subsoil to the surface.

The above amounts are a minimum – the more that can be dug in, the better.

Fertilizers

General fertilizers can be added to the soil when it is being prepared. With a sandy soil this is a good idea, but with a clay soil it is not necessary. The danger is that if the fertilizer is broadcast widely it will encourage weeds and unnecessary growth on herbaceous perennials. If you want to add fertilizer, mix some bonemeal with the soil when you are planting trees and shrubs.

Chapter 8

Containers

No garden is complete without at least one group of containers. They can be used to add instant colour and can be removed if they don't look right, or once their flowering season has finished. Plants that are tender, or require a different soil from that in the main garden, can also be accommodated. They will add instant height and maturity to a new garden and provide effective focal points.

Containers are not without problems, but, as with everything in the garden, careful planning and preparation at the outset can keep these down to an acceptable level. The main problem is watering. Being above ground, the soil will dry out more quickly than in the open garden, a problem which can be most acute on hot windy days. Although there is no escape from watering, there are some steps you can take to retain the moisture for as long as possible.

❀ **Terracotta containers can fit in with almost every garden style and setting.**

Choosing containers

Terracotta

The curious thing about terracotta is that it fits in well with so many different styles of garden and, despite its colour, never jars against any colour or variety of flower. It is porous, holding moisture in the summer, which helps to keep the roots of the plants cool, and remaining warm in winter to protect them from the cold.

There are two types of terracotta currently available: the traditional warm terracotta and a more dusty-coloured version recently introduced from the Mediterranean. This new dusty-coloured terracotta is achieved by mixing the terracotta clay with limestone and firing it in woodburning kilns, or in some cases burning old olive pressings.

There is often a problem with the hardiness of terracotta. Ensure that what you

creative gardening for busy people

✿ **Reconstituted stone containers have many uses. Here, one has been turned into a fine bubble fountain.**

✿ **Unusual containers make an immediate impact. This head, by Fairweather Sculpture, is made from a heavy bronze resin to ensure that it is frostproof.**

buy is frost-hardy and protect the pots by pulling them in close to a warm house, or a free-standing wall. Check for cracks, especially around the drainage hole in the bottom. With traditional-coloured terracotta look for containers with a dark colour, which indicates that they have been in the kiln longer and are therefore harder. The dusty-coloured terracotta is handmade, using a tougher material which is reliably frost-hardy.

Concrete and reconstituted stone

These usually come in classical shapes, and there are also some painted or glazed ones. Frost-hardy, and kind to the plant roots, these containers ought to be more widely used and accepted. The problem is that the walls are fairly thick, leaving the soil area comparatively small unless the container is of sufficient size. This often makes them large, clumsy and difficult to move.

Metal

The earliest metal containers to appear in gardens were old lead water tanks that had come to the end of their useful life. These urns are highly decorated, and fine examples can be seen at Knighthayes Court in Devon. There are modern copies available, which are very effective and may be the perfect solution for a period garden.

They are frost-hardy, but plants do not do as well as in alternative containers.

Plastic

The 'cinderella' of container materials. It is not as bad as it sounds as long as you choose from one of the good-quality copies of traditional material. The advantage of plastic is that it is lightweight, hardwearing and possibly cheaper than other materials. It is not as kind to plants as terracotta or reconstituted stone, and will need to have a drainage hole drilled into the bottom. It is essential to use plastic containers on a balcony or roof garden.

Pottery and stoneware

It is possible to obtain some outstanding one-off pieces of pottery from garden shows and craft fairs. It is a great way to ensure that your garden stands out and has an element of your own personality imprinted upon it. Ensure that the piece has been designed for use outside and is therefore frost-hardy.

Keeping plants alive in containers

Hot weather

Smaller containers hold less soil and will dry out more quickly than larger ones. Terracotta, concrete and similar materials will help to insulate the root ball, keeping it cool in summer and warm in winter – they will also soak up and hold some of the moisture. Non-porous containers, made from plastic or metal, are less kind and will dry out faster.

A soil-based compost will dry out more slowly than a peat-based (or an environmentally friendly substitute) one, but is much heavier and will make the container more difficult to move. Your choice should be based on whether the container is to be mobile, and this may be determined by its size. If it is going to be permanently placed, use a soil-based compost (something like John Innes no. 2 or 3), otherwise go for a lighter, peat-based alternative. Mixing peat- and soil-based composts creates a mixture that is lighter but still has some water-retaining properties – a compromise which may be useful in certain instances.

There are various things you can add to the compost to help it to retain water. These are fairly effective, acting like small sponges which soak up water at watering time and making it available to the plants over an extended period. Some come in the form of a gel, which swells on contact with water, others are made up of tiny pieces of polystyrene, and there are even natural materials like vermiculite.

If the container is in full sunlight, or exposed to the prevailing wind, it will dry out more quickly than onc in a sheltered spot. If drying out is a problem, consider giving it some protection in hot or windy weather, in the form of some shade or a windbreak. Smaller containers can be moved to a shady spot until the conditions improve.

Plants that cope best with dry conditions tend to originate from areas of the world which have a warm, arid climate. Any plant with grey foliage will have originated from a hot country and will hold up well. Herbs are very good: the oils, which we value for flavouring our food, are useful to the plant in that they evaporate more slowly than water and so make the plant more drought-resistant. Plants such as cistus and scented-leafed pelargoniums are not generally regarded as herbs, but they also have oil in

✿ **This group of three containers, in a garden designed by Geoff Whiten, would look good without any plants.**

their veins, giving them a distinctive scent when their leaves are crushed.

Watering

Watering should be carried out regularly, ideally once a day and twice for hanging baskets or on hot days. Rain does not do the watering for you but it can slow the drying process down, so check the condition of the soil after rain by pressing a finger into the top of the compost.

Irrigation systems are now available at most garden centres and these are particularly effective for containers, especially hanging baskets. A timed valve can also be attached to ensure that the watering is carried out even when you are not there.

Cold weather

Cold can be just as much of a problem for containers as heat. In the open ground roots are tucked up under a layer of soil which, in normal conditions, insulates them, keeping them warm and ensuring that they do not freeze. In containers, however, the soil is above the ground, offering less protection from the cold. Choosing a solid container made of concrete or clay can help, as these offer some insulation. The problem is caused by the soil freezing solid; when this happens the plant cannot take up nutrients and it will die in the same way as if watering is neglected in the summer. A simple solution is to move the containers close to a warm house wall. The wall will be heated by the sun during the day and give out heat overnight to help ensure that the plants survive. This is usually sufficient, but wrapping the pots in hessian or insulating fleece (available at every garden centre) will add extra protection.

Container gardening for effect

Containers always look better in groups. On my travels I frequently come across paved areas or paths, which are cluttered by single

✿ **This urn, at Hestercombe in Devon, has been used as a centrepiece for a planting scheme; it acts like the hub of a wheel, with the plants revolving around it. Compare it with the identical urn in the background which has a more formal, statuesque appearance. The character of each piece has been changed by its position within the garden.**

containers dotted about, and simply pulling these containers together into odd numbered groups is an immediate change which can have quite a dramatic effect. In fact, a group of three containers, of different sizes, always looks good, even when plantless (which also has the advantage of being maintenance-free). Positioned in an out-of-the way corner of the patio, or as the centrepiece of a planting scheme, the group will become a highlight of the garden.

If you have a lot of small nondescript containers, perhaps ordinary flowerpots planted with summer colour, pull them all together into a large group and add a slightly larger container as a centrepiece. This larger container should be planted with a spiky plant such as a cordyline or phormium (bamboo if the group is in shade); the dramatic upward thrust of the new plant will contrast with the other shapes in the group.

In more formal settings, use single containers to mark key points. Box and bay balls can be used effectively on either side of a doorway; smaller containers and plants on either side of a seat. For this to work, the containers are better in balanced pairs.

A single container can be useful as an alternative to a statue, to act as a focal point or as the centrepiece of a planting scheme. Chimney pots or upright urns work well in the latter setting.

Containers can be effective in a scree bed (see page 100), but they should be used more informally. A single Grecian-type urn lying haphazardly on its side, or two urns, one upright and one lying down, are effective. A carpet of thyme or New Zealand burr (*Acaena microphylla*) and a small grass will complete the scene.

Plants for containers

Rather than give a list of plants suitable for containers, or even a series of 'recipes', I have put together a number of container groupings and the associated plants. This is much easier to manage than planting lots of plants into a single container; if one plant looks poor it can be removed or replaced, the arrangement can be changed periodically, and the plants are easier to maintain when individually planted.

Full sun group

Container 1: 1 x *Cordyline australis*.
3 x *Thymus serpyllum* 'Coccineus'
Container 2: 1 x *Hebe toparia*
Container 3: 1 x *Convolvulus cneorum*
Container 4: 1 x red zonal-leafed pelargonium (this will need replacing annually).
Container 5: 1 x *Thymus serpyllum* 'Annie Hall'

If you look at the shapes of these plants you will see that I have echoed much of what was discussed in Chapter 5. All the shapes within the arrangement will complement each other and will be supported by whites, reds and pinks in the height of the summer. Position the group in full sun, preferably backed by a wall to give some winter protection. These plants are all reasonably drought-resistant, although watering should be carried out every evening, at least, in hot weather.

Alternatives:

1: *Phormium tenax* 'Maori Sunrise' 2: *Hebe* 'Mrs Winder' 3: *Potentilla* 'Manchu' 4: Fuchsia 'Winston Churchill' 5: Red ivy-leafed pelargonium.

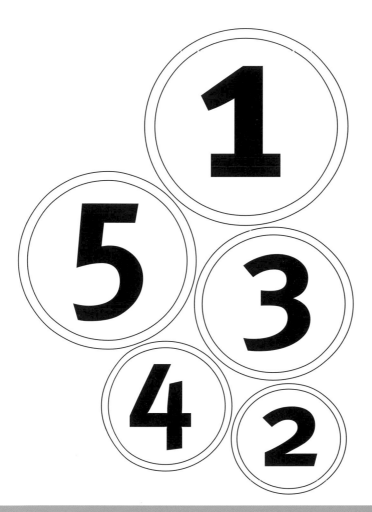

✿ **Container plan.**

Again drought-resistant, but the fuchsia will need an extra daily water. The fuchsia and pelargonium will need replacing annually.

1: *Yucca gloriosa* 2: *Potentilla* 'Tilford Cream' 3: *Anthemis* 'E.C. Buxton' 4: *Rosmarinus* 'Severn Seas' 5: *Thymus lanuginosus*.

This grouping is probably the most drought-resistant, although you should still not neglect the watering.

Shady group

Container 1: 1 x *Fargesia nitida*
Container 2: 1 x *Lysimachia nummularium* (creeping Jenny – a fairly invasive trailing plant, but perfect in a container)
Container 3: 1 x *Dryopteris filix-mas*
Container 4: 1 x *Hosta fortunei albopicta*
Container 5: 1 x *Buxus sempervirens*, clipped to a ball

Again, the shapes of leaf and plant have

been paramount in this grouping. However, it is essential that the group is placed in a shady, protected spot. *Hosta fortunei* is the best variety of hosta for containers. Definitely not drought-resistant and will require watering each day in hot weather.

Alternatives

1: *Camellia* 'Donation'
2: *Pieris japonica*
3: *Osmanthus delavayi*
4: *Gaultheria procumbens*
5: *Vinca minor* 'Atropurpurea'

This grouping contains three plants which either need or prefer an acid soil, so ensure that containers 1, 2 and 4 are filled with ericaceous compost and ideally water the plants with rainwater. If rainwater is difficult to obtain, leave tap water in a bucket, or another similar container, for two or three days, after which most of the hardness will have gone; an alternative would be to add sequestered iron (available at any garden centre) to the water.

Camellia flowers can be damaged by early morning sun, so avoid an east-facing position. Tougher than the first choice, but still not drought-resistant.

1: *Fatsia japonica* 2: *Deschampsia caespitosa* 3: *Alchemilla mollis* 4: *Bergenia cordifolia* 'Silberlicht' 5: *Waldsternia ternata*.

Any type of soil this time, but again not disease-resistant.

✿ **This Russian vine** (*Fallopia baldschuanica*) **has been planted to cover a pergola. However, the restriction of the roots in the container ensures that it will not grow much larger than it is now.**

Climbers in containers

A common problem in gardens occurs where paving, or a hard surface, comes right up to the house wall. The owner wants to grow a climber against the house but he or she is unable, or unwilling, to break into the soil underneath and solves the problem by planting a climber in a container next to the wall.

The trouble is that climbers, in general, are large plants – they have to be if they are to cover walls and fences. In order to reach the height they do requires a fairly substantial, and greedy, root system. In a container these roots quickly fill the container, squeezing out the soil and leaving nothing to hold any moisture; from this moment on the container requires watering several times a day just to keep the plant alive.

The restricted roots also have another effect: they miniaturize the plant, in the same way that a bonsai tree is kept small. This means that where a plant in open ground may cover the side of a house, it will only reach perhaps 1.8 metres (6ft) or even less in a container.

In all cases it is much better to create a hole in the paved area close to the house. This can be done by simply lifting a paving slab and breaking up whatever is underneath or by using a power drill to break through any concrete. If this is really out of the question, perhaps raised beds would be the answer, or something with a sufficient amount of soil to allow the climber to reach its full potential.

Some smaller climbers can be grown in containers – they include *Clematis macropetala*, *C. alpina* and *C. cirrhosa balearica*. There are some miniature climbing roses that would also be suitable.

Mixed containers

So far I have avoided 'recipes' for making up a mixed container – the book is aimed at busy people and this kind of container gardening is high in maintenance. There are, however, some very simple techniques that can be applied.

First, choose a good-sized container, say 60cm (2ft) in diameter across the top. Add crocks, compost, etc. Then select an evergreen garden shrub (ultimate size is not important at this stage). Plant it either in the centre of the container for an all-round display, or close to the back if the container is

to be viewed only from the front. Around its feet plant some summer bedding: perhaps impatiens, trailing petunias, ivy-leafed pelargoniums, lobelia or alyssum. Add a single variegated ivy plant to cascade down one side.

Being evergreen, the shrub will provide colour all the year round. Once the summer bedding has finished, replace it with winter-flowering violas or bellis daisies. In this way the container will provide year-round colour.

Good shrubs for this purpose include: *Viburnum tinus*, *Fatsia japonica*, elaeagnus, sarcococca, *Mahonia japonica* and pieris (this must have an acid compost). The larger shrubs should remain in the container only for a couple of years, after which they can be planted into the open garden and replaced by a new specimen.

Building up a container from scratch

The container should have a drainage hole in the bottom for any excess water to escape. If there isn't one, then make one using a drill (material such as terracotta may be damaged by this treatment, so make sure that any you buy already have drainage holes).

Place some crocks around the hole (these are usually made from broken flowerpots, large flat stones or broken pieces of polystyrene plant container) to ensure good drainage. Add compost (soil- or peat-based) and then the plants, ensuring that the top level of the soil is about 15cm (2in) lower than the rim of the container to aid watering. When watering, fill the space in the top of the container up to the rim. This is a good measure of how much water a container will require in one watering.

91

✿ **Impatiens, ivy-leafed pelargoniums, petunias and trailing lobelia are all reliable plants for hanging baskets.**

Hanging baskets

These popular containers have burst on to the gardening scene in the last twenty years. They can be extremely colourful and are a superb way of brightening a wall or doorway. They are not ideal for the busy person, as they are high in maintenance, but they are so effective that we should look at ways of using baskets while reducing the amount of work involved.

When discussing ground-dwelling containers we looked at the watering problem. With hanging baskets that problem is even more acute. They tend to be much smaller and therefore hold less soil; and, swinging around in mid-air, they are exposed to the full desiccating effects of the wind.

As with other containers, the answer lies in how they are put together. First, select a container with a top diameter of at least 35 cm (14in) and ensure that the wiring is open and easy to plant through. Line the base of the basket with moist moss to ensure that the compost does not fall out. There are many man-made alternatives to moss, but none of them look as good or are as effective. Place a circle of plastic (a piece cut from the compost bag would be fine), or a plastic saucer, in the base to ensure that water does not fall straight through the bottom of the container.

Use a peat-based compost (or environmentally friendly alternative) – soil-based will be too heavy – and mix some water-retaining granules with it. Bring the moss up the side of the basket to the level of the first set of holes and add compost to the same level. Plant trailing plants through the holes in the container, add more moss around the side, then build the compost up to the next layer of planting. Continue with this until the moss reaches the top of the basket and then extend it about 2.5cms (1in) above the rim. Stop the compost about 2.5 cm (1in) from the top of the container, forming a dish in the top. The lip of the moss and the dish in the compost will help to hold the water in the centre of the basket long enough for it to soak in, avoiding the common problem of the water running down the sides without getting to the central root-ball.

Once the basket is completed, hang it on a bracket so that the container is at eye level – too high and you are looking at the underside, too low and the trailing plants are not appreciated.

Despite all these precautions, a hanging basket will require watering twice a day in the height of the summer. If you are not around to carry out the necessary watering, or if the conditions are very severe (strong wind can be devastating), take the basket down and store it out of the wind and sun, returning it when more clement conditions return.

Herbs have been mentioned before, and they are excellent for hanging baskets. Try filling one with culinary herbs and hanging it by the kitchen door. Replant it each spring, as plants become too large for the basket.

Roof gardens and balconies

Containers can be very useful on roof gardens or balconies, where it is extremely difficult to create a garden in the same way as at ground level. The big difference with this type of gardening is in the weight, so lightweight materials such as plastic must be used. This is not as bad as it sounds – there are some very good plastic containers available and sometimes it is difficult to tell them from the real thing. You should also use peat-based compost, or a good peat substitute, and pieces of broken polystyrene for the drainage crocks.

Chapter 9

Hobby Gardening

The last thing a busy person wants is to increase the amount of time they need to spend working in the garden. Many people, however, do just that by incorporating a feature such as a pond or greenhouse, or by aspiring to something beyond their capability, like a 'bowling-green' lawn. Quite unwittingly a sub-set of the garden can take on a life of its own, requiring dedication and application usually reserved for an occupation or hobby.

I am not suggesting that you should not incorporate any of these features in your garden, in fact some can be very rewarding, but you should do so with your eyes open. The following sections include advice to help keep the work to a minimum and suggest alternative approaches.

Water gardening

By this I mean anything within the garden which centres around water, from a lake right down to a simple boggy patch of soil.

A small open pond is perhaps one of the most difficult things to deal with. It can fill with blanket weed, freeze so solidly in the winter that the fish, and wildlife, die, and offers an easy meal to a passing heron.

Algae (of which blanket weed is a form) is nature's way of tidying things up. She doesn't like waste, regarding an open stretch of water, combined with excess sunlight, as being just that, and will proceed to use up the excess. She does this with algae – try leaving a bucket of water on the patio and see how long it takes to turn green. The best way to stop algae, therefore, is to shade the pond and ensure that any excess water and sunlight are used up. This can be achieved by introducing plants with floating leaves, such as water-lilies, to shade the water, and using plenty of submerged, or oxygenating, plants. The aim is to get the balance right between the amount of sunlight getting into the pond and the planting, without clogging it up with foliage or allowing an excess of sunlight. This can be difficult and involves a lot of dedication. The larger the pond the easier it will be, as nature will play a helping hand and small amounts of algae are less noticeable.

✿ **A large stretch of water will quickly settle into a balanced existence and will look after itself, as long as invasive plants like bulrush or reed mace are kept out.**

✿ **A simple bubble fountain can easily be created by drilling a hole through a rockery stone. This one was created by designer Geoff Whiten.**

One warning. Within a few days of filling a pond with fresh tap water the water will go a pea-soup-green colour. This is caused by algae feeding on the salts in the hard water and will clear in time. If you panic and put in fresh water the process will begin again.

Ice can be a serious problem in small pools. Plant and animal detritus collects at the bottom of every pond and gives off noxious gases as it decays. Ice can completely cover a small pond so that these gases cannot escape. They collect under the ice and poison not just the fish but other animals such as frogs which hibernate in the mud at the bottom. In a large pond the volume of water is sufficient to absorb the gases, but in a small pond it can be deadly. If you can keep a hole in the ice this should solve the problem, but the only effective ways are costly, and floating a ball on the surface doesn't work – it ends up rolling about on the ice. A water pump just under the surface can keep the water clear, but it must be kept running throughout the cold weather. The pond heaters available at most garden or aquatic centres are also effective.

Herons have become a serious pest in recent years and, short of covering the surface with mesh, there are no really good ways of stopping them feeding at a pond. None of the usual suggestions work, such as model

creative gardening for busy people

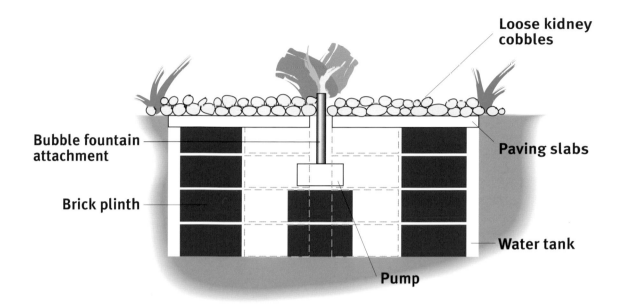

Loose kidney cobbles

Bubble fountain attachment

Paving slabs

Brick plinth

Water tank

Pump

herons, low wire fences and drainage pipes for the fish to hide in. Koi carp keepers prefer very deep ponds with straight sides, and this seems to be reasonably effective, although it can be difficult to see the fish. My solution is to make the pond as deep as possible, introduce drainage pipes (painted black to disguise them) into the bottom, and buy only small, inexpensive fish. In this way, any losses can be replaced reasonably cheaply. If any fish survive an attack, they will be wiser and perhaps live longer as a result.

An alternative to a small pond with fish is one purely for wildlife, which can be any size. Fill it with water-loving plants such as water-lilies, water iris and marsh marigolds and hide it at the back of a border where it will soon attract frogs, toads and newts. This type of pond will require little work, though it will still need to be kept free of ice in the winter in case frogs are hibernating in it, and may need topping up with water in the summer.

If you simply want water which is hassle-free, there are some viable alternatives. The most obvious and perhaps the most rewarding is the bubble fountain. Water bubbles through or over something, for example a stone, and returns to an underground reservoir from where a pump recirculates it. This type of fountain is very easy to construct and you can incorporate all kinds of features. Place it close to the sitting area, where the sound can best be enjoyed.

One warning: there is a lot of evaporation from a bubble fountain, a lot more then anyone expects. Submersible pumps must operate under water or they will be damaged, so make sure they don't dry out. You need a substantial reservoir under the ground or you may find yourself adding water to the fountain on a daily basis. The best solution is to install a 25-gallon water tank (available at builder's merchants). There are some bubble fountain kits on sale with a reservoir which is far too small, so choose carefully.

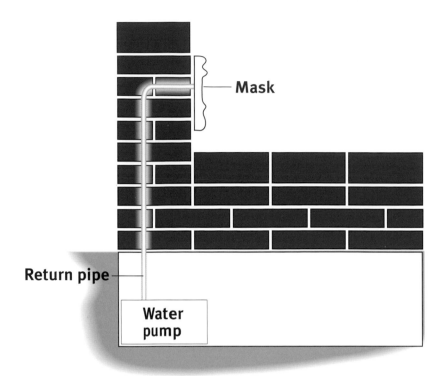

Mask

Return pipe

Water
pump

✿ **A mask fountain.**

An extension to the bubble fountain is the mask fountain. A wall is constructed through which the water is passed, jetting out from a wall mask or over a waterfall. As with the bubble fountain, a substantial reservoir is required to ensure that the pump does not dry out, but in this case a stretch of open water is desirable.

Bog gardens

Bog gardens can be pleasant features, but again they require some attention. A bog garden is one where the soil is kept moist but not waterlogged, and this moisture must be maintained or the plants will dry out and possibly die. You can achieve this by installing a piece of pond liner under a stretch of ordinary garden soil (it works best on clay soils). The pond liner should be pierced in places to allow any excess water to escape.

Rockery waterfalls and rills

The secret to a successful rock garden and any associated waterfall is to make it look as natural as possible. In areas of the country where these things do not occur naturally, they nearly always look contrived, so take care before proceeding. The main problem is leaks, which can appear at any time and take a lot of finding.

Make sure the pool at the bottom of the run is larger than the one at the top (the header pool). This is important when the pump is switched off and the water drains through the system. Butyl liners can look unsightly – use either waterproof concrete or fibreglass.

A rill is a good alternative to a rock waterfall and will combine well with a simple bubble fountain and a scree bed. The idea is to simulate a very small stream bubbling up

✿ **Narrow streams or rills are good ways of adding moving water while retaining a natural feel.**

The rockery in itself is not a problem for the busy gardener – the problems come along as the feature develops, and the main one is the selection of plants. It is not uncommon to buy a dozen rock plants from a garden centre only to find, twelve months later, that one or two of those plants have swamped the whole area. This is the first lesson. Every plant purchased for a miniature garden must be thoroughly investigated to make sure that it is the right size for where it is to be used. This is good advice for the whole garden, but with alpines it is absolutely essential.

Many of the smaller alpines also require specialist attention. The usual problem is with moisture collecting around the centre, or rosette, of the foliage, which causes the plants to rot and eventually die. Experts will either suspend a piece of glass over the plant to prevent water from landing on it or grow it in a specialist greenhouse; this is usually an ordinary greenhouse with side panels removed to allow air in but no rain. Obviously this type of gardening should be left to the serious alpine gardener, but nevertheless it is important for the busy gardener to identify the troublesome plants and avoid them. Lewisias, for example, have an eye-catching display in the spring, making them an ideal subject for the garden centre to tempt us with. They can be grown at

from a natural spring. As long as the garden has a small slope, it can be a very effective way of introducing water to the garden.

Alpine Gardening

By alpine gardening, I mean gardening with miniature plants. To many of us this means building a rockery, and this usually occurs in a garden as a result of the addition of a new pond; the excavated soil is mounded up, dotted with rocks and planted with a collection of alpines bought haphazardly from the garden centre.

an angle between rocks where the rainwater runs off them, but I have still found it difficult to keep them alive. Drabas also suffer from this rotting off, and are commonly on sale in garden centres. I recommend buying alpines from a specialist nursery, where the correct information on growing them can be obtained.

The name 'alpine' suggests that the plants like to grow on a mountainside, so to accommodate this we try to create a miniature mountain. This stops us thinking of other ways to grow them, many of which are more effective and less troublesome. They are very versatile and can be grown in numerous different settings. So, for now, let us forget about rockeries and explore other ways of using these wonderful little plants.

The scree bed

Scree, or loose material on the side of mountains, is probably where many true alpines actually grow in the wild, so in a way we are catering for their needs. In fact 'scree' in a garden is usually a term given to areas of pea shingle designed for planting in rather than walking on. Those plants that tend to overrun a traditional rockery are perfect for this type of environment; they spread out to form a mat and can even cope with being walked on a little.

In relation to the overall garden, the scree bed adds another dimension. It can, just like the true scree on the side of a mountain, be an ever-changing area. Loose cobbles and larger stones, stepping stones and statues, can all be moved around as the mood takes you. Planting can be less rigid than in a border – the plants can be isolated rather than planted to associate with neighbours.

A simple bubble fountain makes a fine addition to a scree bed, where it can be designed to look like a spring bubbling from the ground. For more details see page 97.

Construction of a scree bed could not be simpler, but there are some things to watch out for. Most plants that like to grow in this environment prefer a free-draining soil with the minimum of nutrients, so for clay-based soils you should dig in plenty of sharp sand, but avoid improving

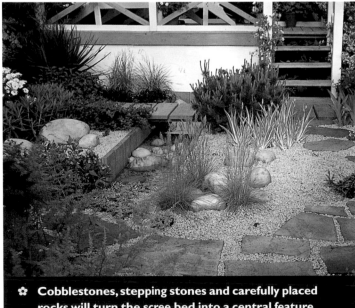

✿ **Cobblestones, stepping stones and carefully placed rocks will turn the scree bed into a central feature within the garden.**

❀ **Small rock plants can be planted directly into tufa, their roots eventually permeating the structure.**

the soil further. There is always a fear of weeds in this type of area, and it is a great temptation to lay the pea shingle over a mulching mat. This can, however, cause a lot more problems than it solves. We are dealing with fairly small plants, so we cannot afford to have the pea shingle too deep or we will not be able to plant into it, while with a mulching mat the pea shingle needs to be fairly deep to hide it. Also, we want the plants to spread across the scree, and even seed themselves and planting through a single hole in the matting will not allow this. Overall, it is much better to lay the shingle and all the other elements of your scree bed straight on to the prepared soil.

Good plants for a scree bed include:

Acaenas
Carex comans 'Bronze Form'
Festuca glauca
F. eskua
Ophiopogon planiscarpus 'Nigrescens'
Taxus baccata 'Repens Aurea'
Thymus serpyllum
Verbascums

Tufa rock

This curious material is, in fact, not a rock but a limestone deposit created by water which has passed though limestone rock. It is very soft and can be carved with a teaspoon, if necessary.

This softness, combined with its high porosity, enables plants to be planted straight into it. Simply carve out a hole, add some alpine planting mixture (two parts potting compost, one part sharp sand and a generous sprinkling of bonemeal), and plant the alpine straight into the hole. Secure with a thin dibber, or the wrong end of a pencil. As time goes by the roots of the plant will force their way through the tufa, eventually requiring no soil at all. One third of the rock should be buried into soil or a pile of sand to assist the capillary action of water, which the tufa will suck up and which is essential for the plants. Always water the soil or sand around the base of the tufa and not straight on to the rock or plants.

✿ **A stone sink is a fine way of displaying smaller alpines. Here, house-leeks and phlox are combined with an interesting arrangement of stone.**

Tufa is fairly easy to obtain through your local garden centre and usually comes in football-sized chunks, which can be planted up and used to decorate a scree bed, large container or patio. As this style of gardening involves the very smallest plants, care must be taken in selecting the right ones. One mistake and the whole arrangement will be spoilt. Any of the following would be fine:

Dianthus 'Pink Jewel'
Erinus alpinus 'Dr Hahnle'
Saxifraga x apiculata
Sedum spathulifolium 'Capo Bianco'

Once planted, a tufa garden requires little maintenance apart from regular watering in dry weather.

Sink Gardens

Miniature gardens can also be created in stone sinks. Once established, a sink requires little work apart from watering, and can be turned into a central feature of the garden. From a design point of view I like to see them in groups of three, but a single specimen can also make a fine display. Most of the flowering occurs in the spring, so make sure it is placed where it can be seen at that time of the year. A traditional stone sink can be difficult to find these days, but not impossible. There are also companies who make new ones from hollowed-out stone (usually Yorkstone).

Ensure that your sink has a drainage hole (in a traditional sink this will be provided by the old plug-hole). Place some crocks or loose gravel over the bottom to aid drainage, and fill the container with alpine planting mixture. Place a small piece of flat-topped stone, or tufa off-cut, towards one corner and plant a miniature upright conifer behind it to add solidity to the design. Plant trailing plants around the edge and some cushion-forming alpines in the centre.

The plants used for stone sinks can be larger than those recommended for tufa but care must still be exercised in their selection. If in doubt, choose from those listed for tufa or from the following:

Conifer
Juniperus communis compressa

Trailing
Artemisia schmidtiana 'Nana'
Phlox subulata

Cushion-forming
Armeria juniperifolia alba
A. maritima 'Dusseldorf Pride'
Dianthus 'La Bourboule'
Primula 'Snow Cushion'
Saxifraga 'Esther'
S. 'Kathleen Pinsent'
S. x elisabethae 'Primrose Dame'
S. 'Silver Cushion'
S. 'Whitehills'

Finish the container off with a layer of sharp grit, carefully working it under the foliage of each plant. This will protect the delicate leaves from any splashback during watering or rain.

Fruit and vegetables

Gardens originally developed around the need to supply food and medicines, and it was only later that the ornamental side became appreciated. Even today there are people who believe that no garden is complete without fruit and vegetables.

✿ **Vegetable gardens are high in maintenance, but the results can be very rewarding.**

There is certainly nothing to compare with fresh produce straight out of the garden, but it should not be undertaken by anyone who does not have the time.

Vegetables

The majority of vegetables are annuals or biennials, or are treated as such, which means that the vegetable patch has to be dug up and replanted every year. Vegetables are greedier than many other plants, so the ground will need a thorough feeding when dug over, usually incorporating well-rotted manure or compost at the same time. Most vegetable plants are susceptible to pests and diseases, and you will need to deal with these otherwise the crop may be destroyed. Weeding, feeding and picking will all need to be done regularly.

Some vegetables can be grown in the garden with the minimum amount of effort. They will produce a reasonable crop, which will be increased if you dig in well-rotted organic matter in the spring. The following is a list of the more ornamental varieties.

Asparagus

This perennial is harvested when the shoots are young, which is only for a short time. After this the shoots develop into tall feathery fronds, attractive in the border and when picked for the house. To produce really good-quality asparagus involves a lot of feeding and cultivating, but even without this you will have an edible crop.

Artichokes

By this I do not mean the Jerusalem artichoke, which is an invasive thug, but the globe artichoke (*Cynara scolymus*). It is a large grey-leafed architectural plant, perfect for the back of a warm sunny border. The flower-heads can be cut during the summer for use in the kitchen.

Aubergines, tomatoes and gourds (marrows etc.)

These tender plants usually need to be grown in the greenhouse for a good crop, but they can also be grown in open ground. The flowers of aubergines are large, round and

✿ **Aubergine flowers can be spectacular. This one is called 'Ova'.**

lilac in colour – good in the mixed border. The fruits of tomatoes, especially the small ones, can be an unusual and colourful addition. Fruits can be white, yellow or orange, as well as red.

Gourds and marrows can be treated as climbers and grown up a frame or a small fence.

French and runner beans
Runner beans were originally grown for their bright red flowers; it was not until later that people realised that the pods were edible. Sow in small pots and transplant the young plants into their growing position. Try 'Painted Lady', which has attractive red and white flowers, or 'Ruby Moon', which has lilac flowers and purple backs to its leaves.

Cabbages
There are a number of ornamental coloured cabbages available and they are quite often used in winter bedding schemes. I have not tried them, but I am told they are tough and need more cooking than ordinary ones.

Carrots
The feathery foliage of carrots associates well in the mixed border. They can be grown from seed or sown in situ.

Ruby chard
This has an almost luminous scarlet stem that stands out in any planting scheme.

Rhubarb
As a garden plant, rhubarb has a lot to recommend it. It has pleasing red stems

✿ **Dwarf French beans can be used effectively as a border edging.**

✿ **Rhubarb is a perennial which makes a good 'spot' plant in a planting scheme.**

✿ **Foliage shape and texture, coupled with flower and fruit colour, can make an attractive display. Here, cabbage 'Black Tuscany', beetroot 'Macgregor's Favourite', runner bean 'Czar' and tomato 'Tiny Tim' create a pleasing effect.**

✿ **Apple trees come in a range of shapes and sizes. This 'Spartan' apple has been trained as a 'step-over' cordon, making it a perfect addition to the mixed border.**

topped by large flat leaves and will also grow in a bog garden. It makes a fine addition to the mixed border, as long as you can ignore visitors' comments.

Fruit Trees

Unlike vegetables, it is possible to have fruit from your own garden without having to put in any work at all.

Apples

In some ways apples are one of the easiest trees to grow; in others they can be quite time-consuming. Techniques for tree-growing are now extremely sophisticated, and it is possible to choose between a plant which will grow to a mere 1.2 m (4ft) in height and one which will reach up to 4m (13ft) plus. They can be trained against a wall or grown in a large container on a patio, although this will restrict their growth and reduce the crop. The size that the plant grows to is decided by the rootstock, which will have been specially developed to control the tree size. Decide the size and shape of plant you want before you order it, and obtain it from a specialist fruit grower who will be able to ensure that you get something that is suitable. See *The Plant Finder* or look in the back of one of the many gardening magazines for details of growers.

Once you have decided on the size, select a variety that you like. An apple tree will require a pollinator, which is basically another apple tree, or crab apple, which flowers at the same time, and this will have to be planted close by. It is possible to buy trees which have limbs of a pollinator grafted on, in an effort to produce a self-pollinating plant, but with these you may not have the same choice of varieties. Some apple varieties, notably 'Jonagold' and 'Blenheim Orange', are what is know as triploid. This means that they are poor pollinators and require two other varieties close by, instead of one, to ensure good results. I would avoid these.

Apple trees can last for many decades, and many gardens already have an old tree. It may have a gnarled trunk and a good shape, which contributes to the look of the garden, regardless of its fruit. Unless there are severe problems, or the tree is in totally the wrong place, an apple is well worth keeping as part of a new design. Fallen fruit can create some difficulty in the autumn, but as long as herbaceous plants, which die down in the winter, are used under the tree, this will not be a great problem. Alternatively, lawn and naturalized spring bulbs can make a fine display as well as being a practical solution. Lawns can be a problem around trees (see page 34), so cut a circle out of the lawn close to the trunk and plant an aggressive geranium like *Geranium endressii* or *G. macrorrhizum* – the plants tend to flower at the same time as the apples, and the circle will restrict their spread.

Remember, just because it is an old tree doesn't mean that it can produce fruit without a pollinator. If you have a pair of trees and remove one, you may lose your apple crop. If you have a tree which suddenly stops producing, it may be that the pollinator was in a garden close by and has been removed. To find a replacement pollinator, note exactly when your tree flowers and consult a specialist nurseryman.

Cherries

The big problem with cherries is their size. A wild cherry is a large woodland tree and even the dwarfing rootstocks of the cultivated varieties still only restrict the tree to 3.5m (12ft) in height, so you need plenty of space. The cherries are much loved by birds, who devour the fruits off the tree while they are still green, so you will need a very large net if you want to guarantee a complete crop. This is obviously impractical, though I have found that simply netting a single branch can provide some fruit.

Taking everything into account, I would not plant a cherry, but if you already have one, enjoy it; it is a haven for wildlife.

Pears

Much of what has been said about apples also refers to pears. You will need to decide the size and shape of tree before ordering, again from a specialist fruit grower. You will not,

✿ **A fan-trained pear can be a fine architectural feature in the garden.**

however, be able to obtain a tree quite as small as that available for an apple.

Pears also need a pollinator close by and, again, some varieties are triploid. They are very long-lived, sometimes up to 200 years, and can make very fine ornamental specimens, especially those trained as fans or espaliers.

Plums

Dwarfing rootstocks for plums have appeared only recently and even then the plants will reach 2.2 metres (8ft) in height. In general they are self-fertile, so only one tree is required, and they have fewer problems with pests and diseases than most other fruiting plants. In fact, for many years I have had a plum tree which receives no attention whatsoever, apart from when the plums are ready to pick. The only difficulties are the attention of wasps to the overripe fruit and the occasional wild sucker.

Victoria plums are still the best. If you want a fruit tree, and have the space but no time, then this is the one for you.

Peaches, nectarines and apricots

These are very much hobby trees. They require a lot of warmth, preferably backed by a south-facing wall, and a rich soil. They also need protection against marauding birds and are more susceptible to pests and diseases.

Mulberries, quince and medlars

The fruit of the mulberry can be eaten direct from the plant, but is an acquired taste, whereas the fruits of the other two need special treatment before they can be eaten (medlars must be rotten before they are palatable). As ornamental trees, they are perfect for the small garden, although mulberry juice stains can be a nuisance on a patio or path. The medlar in particular has a wonderful umbrella shape. They are also very old varieties and would be perfect in a period garden.

Walnuts and sweet chestnuts

These are large trees, putting them into a different category from the other fruiting trees and shrubs discussed here. As ornamental trees they have many high points, for example the glossy foliage of the chestnut and the subtle bark of the walnut. It can take twenty years before a walnut produces fruit, and sweet chestnuts simply do not perform well outside their native Mediterranean climate. Do not grow them for their fruit.

Hazelnuts and filberts

These are large woodland shrubs that require a reasonable amount of space. In larger planting schemes they can be good plants for the back of the border, and are best cut down to the ground completely every five years to maintain health and vigour. Some of the varieties have purple foliage, with lighter-coloured undersides, creating a pleasing effect in a windy position.

Soft fruit

This includes strawberries, blackberries, blackcurrants and gooseberries. They tend to be herbaceous perennials and shrubs and as such reappear each year. Many are attractive in their own right and can be used within a mixed environment, but the problems are the pests which line up for their share. Birds and animals are the main problem, which is why these plants tend to be grown under a fruit cage. Once a fruit cage is erected, growing fruit starts to become a hobby, so I want to look at alternative ways of growing soft fruit.

Strawberries

The strawberry plant is an evergreen herbaceous perennial that spreads by virtue of a surface root system, rooting new plants as it grows. The plant itself has attractive foliage and pleasing white flowers, followed, of course, by red fruits. It looks good at the front of a border, where the trailing strawberries can grow across their surroundings and blur any hard edges. Birds are the biggest problem, especially blackbirds, which cannot resist them. I personally like both bird and strawberry, so would try to live with the problem – if you plant enough there should be plenty to go round. Alpine strawberries, which have much smaller fruit, are a viable alternative and seem to be of less interest to the birds.

Strawberries also look good trailing over the sides of containers and hanging baskets – in fact there is a special container with small holes in the sides created just for them.

Blackcurrants

I have grown these in a mixed planting scheme and they have proved very effective. The shape of the shrub (it grows to about 90cm (3ft) in height with a similar spread) is pleasing, the foliage attractive and the flowers and fruit a fine addition to the border. 'Ben Sarek' is one of the best varieties for mixed

✿ **Fruit cage**

planting schemes as it is compact, frost- and mildew-resistant, and crops well when planted close together.

Pruning will be needed once the plant is established. One third of the old growth should be removed in October, as is normal with most established deciduous shrubs.

Redcurrants and whitecurrants

I have not found these good for mixed planting unless they are trained up a wall at the back of a sunny border. This is a lot of work, and they are best left to the hobby gardener. If you want to have a go, however, plant the redcurrant 'Yonkheer Van Tets', which is best grown as a cordon. For whitecurrants plant 'White Versailles'.

Gooseberries

These are excellent plants for the mixed border. The foliage is attractive and the plant has a good shape. The fruit is either red or white and creates a pleasing effect in the border even if you do not intend to eat them. They are reasonably idiot-proof, producing a crop even in the worst conditions. If you grow only one soft fruit, this should be it.

The problem with gooseberries is mildew, so plant a variety which is resistant. The best, by far, is 'Invicta'. For red fruits, plant 'Whinham's Industry', which is extremely tolerant and will even grow in shade.

Raspberries, loganberries, tayberries and blackberries

These are the so-called cane fruits. Unless you have space (or a desire) for a bramble patch these fruits are not for you. They produce fruit on the previous year's growth, so in cultivation the exhausted canes are removed and the new growth is tied into specially made frames. It is a lot of work and best left to the hobby gardener. If left alone, an impenetrable briar patch will be created similar to that of blackberries in a hedgerow; not desirable in the small to medium-sized garden.

Grapes

Forget the grapes – the host vine is a perfect addition to any garden. The foliage is attractive, colouring up well in the autumn and it will even grow in poor conditions under trees. If you want grapes, plant the vine against a south-facing wall where the heat will produce the best crop – though this involves careful pruning at the right time. Left alone, however, there will still be some grapes to pick in late summer.

Try 'Boscoop Glory' or 'Fragola'. The latter is commonly known as the strawberry grape, because of its unusual flavour, and is probably the best for producing crops on an untended plant. For growing simply as an ornamental try 'Brant', which has the best foliage.

Figs

As a free-standing plant or trained as a climber, the fig is an excellent, large deciduous garden shrub. It must be grown in full sun if the fruit is to ripen, and the roots should be restricted within a 1.8m (6ft) square box sunk into the ground (which is best made with old paving slabs) otherwise it will produce extra foliage at the expense of the fruit.

'Brown Turkey' is the most commonly planted fig, and is still the best.

Greenhouses

It is always a surprise to me how many people want a greenhouse included in the design of their garden, even though they have requested a low-maintenance scheme. When asked why, they respond that they want to grow bedding plants and tomatoes. In a low-maintenance garden there is little scope for bedding plants, and tomatoes are two a penny when ripe. You must have a good reason to add a greenhouse to your garden and it has to be that you want to grow something specific. In other words you want a hobby – there is no such thing as a low-maintenance greenhouse.

If you have decided that a greenhouse is for you, siting is important. Ideally it will be positioned running east to west, to pick up the most sun and not be too shaded. The greenhouse should be as large as you can afford, in both money and space, as the biggest problem is maintaining a constant temperature which is best achieved by having plenty of room for the air to circulate.

In the height of the summer you may need to provide extra shading, and this can be done by using blinds or whitewashing the glass. Another approach is to screen the greenhouse with trellis and grow a deciduous climber up the framework. This will allow

✿ **A four bin system is one of the best ways of making good garden compost (see page 112).**

plenty of light in during winter and spring, but provide some shading in summer. Greenhouses in general are unattractive, so this treatment will also provide some screening.

A pergola is another good way of providing shade (see page 29).

Compost

Well-rotted organic matter is essential for providing plant food and for conditioning the soil. This can be provided in a number of ways, but the principles are the same – the material must have been allowed to rot for a period of time to break it down into a friable material before it can be used.

Most people think this is easy: just dump all the garden rubbish into a heap in the corner of the garden, add some kitchen waste, leave it for a year and then spread it around the plants. Unfortunately they are wrong – making good compost involves a lot of work and dedication. Poor compost is a liability, spreading weeds and disease around the garden. Frankly, although I am in danger of being condemned by the organic gardening lobby, unless you are going to take composting seriously you are better not including a composting area in your new garden.

The key to making good compost is to use a variety of material and to ensure that every part of the heap has received sufficient heat over a long enough period to break it down. Too often I see a circle of chicken wire secreted into a corner of the garden, filled with grass cuttings and a few weeds. Grass is very high in nitrogen and simply breaks down into a black slurry on its own, so it must be combined with other plant or household waste material to be of any use. The heat required to break down organic

material into compost will only be generated at the centre of the heap while that around the edge will be untouched, and this is what causes the problems. The uncomposted material could contain weed seeds and possibly even disease, and these are then spread all around the garden.

A good composting system will involve four bins: one filled with rotting material which is being filled from the top, the second empty but used for turning the mixture, the third filled with composting material and the fourth with compost being taken from the bottom, for use around the garden. Every five to six weeks the composting material must be turned into the empty bin and mixed thoroughly. This is done for the same reason that food in a microwave oven is stirred half-way through cooking, to ensure that the heat is evenly spread.

In a garden which is dedicated to keeping maintenance to a minimum it is doubtful that enough waste plant material, apart from grass cuttings, will be produced to make a composting system viable. This, coupled with the 'hobby-within-a-hobby' effect of composting, means that a composting area will probably take up valuable space. Small plastic bins are now available and these are effective to a point, but you must be aware that the area around the edge is probably not going to be hot enough to break down weed seeds or roots. With these you must either be more circumspect in your choice of material – avoiding seeds and roots – or you must turn the contents as recommended above. To ensure success restrict yourself to kitchen waste, grass cuttings and leaves in equal measure.

If you do not want to include a composting system in your garden, but are still concerned about the environment, contact you local council and see if they can guide you in the direction of a recycling centre where your waste material can be properly dealt with.

Lawns

Cutting the lawn is undoubtedly the biggest job in any garden, and the gardener who wants an easy life will concentrate on reducing this work to a minimum. The problem with a lawn is that it can become an obsession, with enormous amounts of money spent annually on fertilizers and weedkillers in an attempt to achieve the perfect sward. Again, you must ask yourself some questions. Do you want an emerald green lawn with no weeds, or do you simply want a lawn? Daisies, buttercups and clover can be quite charming in the height of summer.

If you want a lush green sward it is possible, without going to great expense in money and manpower. The best solution is to maintain the lawn at a height of no less than 4 cm (1.5 in) and to mow it more often – perhaps two or three times a week in ideal growing conditions. If some care has been taken in the design of the area (see Chapter 3), this should not be too painful. Leave the collecting box off, as the small grass cuttings will help to nourish the lawn.

Your lawn will become stronger and more aggressive by this method, making it difficult for moss and weeds to gain a foothold. Most problems with lawns stem from cutting them too short, which weakens the grass and allows moss and weeds to develop. Prevention is better than cure, and this solution will only *maintain* a good, or near perfect, lawn. If your lawn is currently overrun by moss and weeds, you should consider re-turfing or reseeding the area and starting again from scratch.

Once you have settled into this cutting regime, the only other work required will be a top dressing of fertilizer in the spring and again in the autumn (do not use a spring lawn fertilizer in the autumn, or vice versa).

Note: There are two other common causes of lawn problems. First, cutting the lawn when it is wet; try to avoid this unless it becomes absolutely necessary. Second, walking on it during the winter months; this can severely weaken and even kill areas. If you find that you need to keep walking across it for access, then make a path (see page 32).

Creating a lawn

Laying turf is the best method, but it is also possible to create a good lawn using seed.

Turf can be laid at any time of the year, depending on the weather (in severely dry or cold conditions the growers will stop cutting the turf). For best results with seed, sow in July or August and cover with a sprinkling of sharp sand (this may sound like a strange time of year, but extensive field trials have proved this to be the perfect timing and method).

Before sowing or turfing, the ground must be carefully prepared. Ideally preparation starts in the autumn, when the area should be dug over; in the spring it should be raked over and carefully consolidated. Consolidation cannot be carried out with a roller, as this will leave air pockets and 'soft' spots, so you must use the tried and tested method of heel and toe, which involves shuffling across the area with your feet close together and your weight on your heels and toes pointed up.

Once the area has been consolidated, rake across it until a fine tilth has been created. It is now ready for sowing or turfing.

113

Plants

Key to codes

Availability
☑ **Easily obtainable. Should be available anywhere.**
▢ **May require some searching or could be seasonal, but should not be too difficult to find.**
▣ **Best to order from a specialist nursery.**

Conditions **Sun or shade**
✳ **Shade**
✳ **Part shade**
✳ **Full sun**

The following pages contain lists of plants which have proved to be reliable, easy to grow and good value: shrubs, herbaceous perennials, trees, bulbs and climbers. The height and spread shown are the expected dimensions after eight years, although this can vary dramatically depending upon the conditions and the age of the plant when planted. Height is given first, followed by spread.

The flowering time indicated represents that of an average year. Some plants are seriously affected by the seasons and can flower up to two months earlier in extreme conditions or be delayed by poor weather.

Bedding Plants

The bedding scheme is perhaps the most noticeable legacy of the Victorian period, as can be seen in the elaborate schemes still used in many of our public parks. The Victorians were great patrons of the plant hunters who were sent out to scour the world, returning with ever more exotic species which were then displayed to impress friends and neighbours. Many of these plants were too tender for our climate, but they could be grown outside during the warm summer months and so the bedding idea was born. Over time it developed into ever more elaborate and wondrous arrangements – sometimes, to impress friends, whole beds would be changed a number of times throughout a single day!

The spring bedding plant bonanza is still an important part of the nursery and garden centre year, proving that this method of gardening is still very much with us. But why do we buy them? Is it just from habit or do we have other reasons? Tastes in gardening vary, and I would not suggest that you should never include a traditional bedding scheme in your garden. But you should be aware that this type of gardening is expensive, time consuming and perhaps not the best way of creating a colourful display. Bedding plants are useful, however, for filling in around developing plants and are ideal for container gardening.

Unless you give regular attention to your bedding plants throughout the summer, the scheme will have a disappointingly short flowering season. In the right conditions most bedding plants will flower all summer long. Many are annuals, living for only the one season, during which time their aim is to flower and produce as many seeds as possible. This prolific flowering makes them useful in many ways, but it uses up a lot of energy, so feeding is essential or they will simply burn themselves out. Before planting, the ground needs good preparation, with

plenty of manure or compost dug into the surface and a general, slow-release, high potassium fertilizer incorporated. Feed with a liquid fertilizer once a week and make sure that the plants do not dry out. Some plants, notably the annual sweet peas, give up flowering once they have set seed and will require regular dead-heading to keep them going.

Do not be stingy when planting bedding plants. Bare soil should disappear, so you will need a plant every 10 or 12 cm (4 or 5 ins). Work out your design beforehand to ensure that the plants are in scale and the colours work together.

Useful bedding plants

Impatiens (Busy Lizzie)
Excellent in either sun or shade, and will cope in the poorest of soils. If short of water they complain by drooping badly, giving time for the lazy gardener to rescue them. Good in containers and will flower all summer.

Nicotiana (Tobacco plant)
The sweet heady scent of this plant on a summer evening makes it an all-time favourite. The only problem is height, as it can reach 60–90cm (2–3 ft) high and look fairly ragged. Dwarf varieties are now available, but these are less scented.

Pelargonium
Often called geranium, but not to be confused with the hardy perennial geraniums, commonly called cranesbills (see page 118). There are a number of different types of this plant, the most useful being the zonal-leafed varieties and the ivy-leafed or trailing. There are even some with exotically scented leaves. All will grow well in containers, especially hanging baskets.

Herbaceous perennials

The definition of a herbaceous perennial is a plant where no stem rises above the surface of the soil except as a temporary structure lasting a single season. This is a very general definition, as clearly there are herbaceous perennials which maintain their leaves for longer than a season, but it does ensure that everyone understands the difference between these plants and the woody trees and shrubs.

Soil

PH Must have an acid soil
▨ Can cope with a light, dry sandy soil
C Grow well in clay soil
▨ Will grow in any soil, but not damp
◪ Will grow in damp or boggy
conditions

Habit

G Good groundcover –the plant
smothers the soil, stopping seeds
from germinating.
M Some groundcover – the soil is
covered but not enough to stop
germination.
P Poor groundcover – there is a lot of
bare soil around the plant.

Planting times

(these represent the optimum time of
the year to plant – for more details see
page 12)
◪ Spring
▨ Autumn
▩ Summer

Top 100 herbaceous perennials

Acaena microphylla (New Zealand burr)

Horizontal evergreen. This very low-growing plant is the rock gardener's nightmare, as it will quickly envelop most forms of alpine garden. However, its habit makes it perfect for covering and disguising items such as manhole covers or for softening

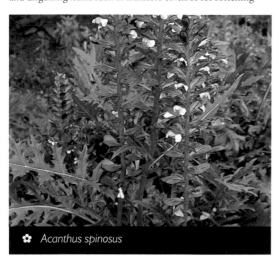

❀ Acanthus spinosus

paving and scree beds. Its evergreen mat is covered in terracotta-coloured burr-shaped flowers in late summer. Underplant with dwarf spring bulbs. 5cm (2in) by 90cm (3ft). Similar varieties: Acaena 'Blue Haze' and A. 'Copper Carpet'.

🔲 ▨ ▨ ▨ C G ◪

Acanthus mollis, A. spinosus (Bear's breeches)

Upright evergreen. This plant has a deep root, making it difficult to move once established. The leaves, which were carved on classical columns and statues, are a fine feature, which is why it is recommended for near the front of a border, but I grow it for the upright flower spikes which stand out well at the back. In shade, it will cover the ground well, but will have few flowers. Always buy large plants where possible, as it appears to be very weak when young. 1.2m (4ft) by 1m (3ft) (spread could be more on a light soil).

☑ ▨ ▨ ✳ ▨ C G ◪

Agapanthus 'Headbourne Hybrids' (African lily)

Spiky deciduous. This spectacular plant is perfect for a warm, sunny, late summer-flowering border. Its blue flowers are held on candelabras at the end of tall stems, above strap-like foliage. Can be reluctant to flower, but thrives on neglect, so try not to pamper it. Agapanthus grow well in containers, but use a smaller pot than you would expect as they flower best in limited space. 60cm (2ft) with a similar spread.

🔲 ▩ ▨ ▨ C P ◪ ▩

Ajuga reptans 'Atropurpurea' (Bugle)

Horizontal evergreen. This ground-covering perennial will spread across the ground in full sun, making it useful close to paving and in scree beds. It has purple foliage topped by blue flower spikes in the spring. It can be a nuisance in some conditions, so must be planted away from less robust perennials. 5cm (2 in) by 90cm (3ft).

☑ ▨ ▩ ▨ ▨ C G ◪

Alchemilla mollis (Lady's mantle)

Woofly deciduous. Its lime-green colours are the perfect foil for many plants, especially roses – planted next to paving it softens and disguises the hard edges. Cut the faded flower heads off to encourage another display. 20cm (8in) with a similar spread.

☑ ▨ ▩ ✳ ▨ ▨ C ◪ G ◪

❀ Alchemilla mollis

Allium christophii

Upright deciduous. This flowering onion has a spectacular, mauve globe-shaped flower atop a tall stem. Grow behind Iris germanica and Sedum 'Ruby Glow', or in front of purple-leafed cotinus. 90cm (3ft) by 30cm (1ft).

▣ ▩ ▨ ▨ C P ◪

Key to codes

Availability
☑ Easily obtainable. Should be available anywhere.
◎ May require some searching or could be seasonal, but should not be too difficult to find.
⬆ Best to order from a specialist nursery.

Conditions **Sun or shade**
❋ Shade
❊ Part shade
❈ Full sun

Anaphalis triplinervis (Pearly everlasting flower)
Woofly deciduous. A tough grey-leafed perennial. Unlike most grey-leafed plants, it is happy in part-shade. Grow with acanthus and bergenias. 40cm (1ft 4in) by 60cms (2ft).

◎ ❊ ❈ ▨ ▣ **C** **M** ◧ ⬛

Anemone × hybrida 'Honorine Jobert'
(Japanese anemone)
Woofly deciduous. Colour in shady spots is difficult to achieve, but this plant can cope with harsh conditions. Large white flowers on tall stems in late summer and early autumn, above attractive feathery foliage which persists throughout the spring and early summer. Can become invasive. 1.5m (5ft) by 60cm (2ft). *Anemone hupehensis* 'Prinz Heinrich' is a shorter pink version.

☑ ❊ ❈ ❋ ▨ ▣ **C** **M** ◧ ⬛

Anthemis tinctoria 'E.C.Buxton'
(Golden marguerite)
Woofly deciduous. This plant, with lemon-yellow daisy-like flowers for most of the summer, is perfect close to a warm sitting area or at the front of a hot sunny mixed border. Looks good with blue or purple delphiniums. 60cm (2ft) with a similar spread.

◎ ❊ ❈ ▨ ▣ **C** **M** ◧ ❈

Artemisia schmidtiana 'Nana'
Woofly evergreen. A low ground-hugging perennial which is good close to the edge of a warm paved area or in a scree bed. Its silver feathery foliage makes a fine foil for the pink flowers of *Geranium cinereum* 'Ballerina'. 5cm (2in) by 45cm (18in).

◎ ❊ ❈ ▨ ▣ **G** ◧

Aruncus dioicus (Goat's beard)
Woofly deciduous. This is another of those plants which, although able to grow in sun or part shade, is so useful for dry shade that it is rarely used for anything else. The foliage is full and feathery, forming a contrast with many evergreen shrubs. The height and spread will vary depending upon the conditions – the height given is for dry shade. It will grow in any soil, even waterlogged. 1.5m (5ft) by 90cm (3ft).

☑ ❊ ❈ ▨ ◫ ▣ **C** **G** ◧

Aruncus dioicus 'Kneiffii' (Goat's beard)
Woofly deciduous. This is a miniature copy of *A. dioicus*. A good alternative to astilbe, which is really only happy in damp conditions. 45cm (18in) by 90cm (3ft).

◎ ❊ ❈ ▨ ◫ ▣ **C** **G** ◧

Astrantia major (Masterwort)
Woofly deciduous. For a plant which dies down every year, this plant offers remarkably good value. The attractive, feathery foliage is topped by unusual green and cream flower heads on the end of wiry stems over a very long period. A superb companion for delphiniums. 60cm (2ft) by 45cm (18in).

☑ ❊ ❈ ▨ ▣ **C** **G** ◧

Astrantia major rubra (Masterwort)
Woofly deciduous. Slightly smaller than the ordinary masterwort, this plant has plum-coloured flowers; otherwise the plants have the same attributes. 45cm (18in) by 30cm (12in).

⬆ ❊ ❈ ▨ ▣ **C** **G** ◧

Bergenia cordifolia 'Purpurascens' (Elephant's ears)
Large-leafed evergreen. This plant is either loved or hated, but used in small groups it can add balance and continuity to a design. Despite being evergreen, it discards older leaves at intervals throughout the year; the dead foliage is easy to recognize and should be removed. The pink flowers appear in early spring and this variety has leaves that turn purple in the winter. 45cm (18in) by 60cm (2ft).

☑ ❊ ❈ ❋ ▨ ▣ **C** **G** ◧

Bergenia cordifolia 'Silberlicht' (Elephant's ears)
Large-leafed evergreen. This plant is identical to 'Purpurascens', but with white flowers and no purple leaf colour in winter. The pink flowers of most bergenias do not combine well with yellows and oranges, but the white flowers of this plant are more forgiving. *B.* 'Bressingham White' is similar.

◎ ❊ ❈ ❋ ▨ ▣ **C** **G** ◧

Brunnera macrophylla
(Chatham Island Forget-Me-Not)
Large-leafed deciduous. A good plant for a woodland setting or where its neighbours are robust enough to cope with its spreading habit. The bright blue forget-me-not flowers appear in April and May, but its main characteristic is the large heart-shaped leaves. 45cm (18in) by 60cm (2ft).

☑ ❊ ❈ ❋ ▨ **C** **G** ◧

Caltha palustris 'Flore Pleno' (Marsh Marigold)
Woofly deciduous. As the common name suggests, this plant grows at the margins of the water garden. Probably best grown in a basket, it brings sunshine to the water garden throughout

spring. In most garden plants the single-flowered species is preferred, but here the double 'Pleno' variety is superior. 30cm (12in) by 45cm (18in).

Carex comans 'Bronze Form' (Sedge)

Spiky evergreen. There is always a concern with grasses that they will become invasive, but, as long as the native *C. pendula* is avoided, the carex are all well-behaved. This one, as the name suggests, has bronze foliage all the year round. Grow with *Alchemilla mollis* and *Heuchera* 'Palace Purple'. 45cm (18in) by 60cm (2ft).

Carex morrowii 'Fisher's Form' (Sedge)

Spiky evergreen. This variegated grass is similar to the more common 'Evergold', but the stripe is more of a creamy white than the yellow. 30cm (12in) with a similar spread.

Carex oshimensis 'Evergold' (Sedge)

Spiky evergreen. Not as refined as 'Fisher's Form' but easier to find. 20cm (8in) by 30cm (12in).

Carex 'Frosted Curls' (Sedge)

Spiky evergreen. Each leaf of this delightful grass has a twist at the end, which creates a cloud-like effect above the leaves. 30cm (12in) with a similar spread.

Corydalis flexuosa

Woofly evergreen. Blue pea-like flowers are held over a mat of feathery foliage. It can be difficult when young, but once established is very effective in providing colour throughout the whole of the summer. 15cm (6in) by 20cm (8in).

Crocosmia masoniorum (Montbretia)

Spiky deciduous. Orange-red flowers are held on long arching stems over grass-like foliage, which appears quite early in the year, adding the spiky leaf shape to any spring display. The flowering season is July and August. Although it is very accommodating, the strong colour of the flowers is best situated in full sun. 90cm (3ft) by 25cm (9 in). *C.* 'Lucifer' is a larger alternative.

Delphinium 'Black Knight', D. 'Galahad', D. 'Blue Jay'

Upright deciduous. There is nothing to compete with the stately delphinium in the summer border, where it adds height and impact. It is the perfect companion for roses, lavender, geraniums, alchemilla and astrantia. Support (a single cane on each flower will suffice) is essential and the work can be a hassle, but the rewards are worthwhile. Always buy named varieties as they have the sturdiest upright stems – avoid the ordinary 'Pacific Strains'. The flowers of 'Black Knight' are dark purple, 'Galahad' white and 'Blue Jay' royal blue with a white centre. Cut the flower stems down to 10cm (4in) above the soil after flowering for a shorter display later in the summer. 1.5–2m (5ft–6ft 6in) by 45cm (18in).

Deschampsia caespitosa (Tufted hair grass)

Spiky evergreen. Native. Flowers appear like a hazy cloud above the solid foliage clump. 90cm (3ft) by 60cm (2ft).

Dicentra formosa 'Luxuriant' (Dutchman's breeches)

Woofly deciduous. Most people know of bleeding heart, or *D. spectabilis*, but it needs a spot out of full sun and becomes rather untidy when it has finished flowering. This plant is smaller, more refined and capable of taking some sun. The flowers are white, appearing in early summer, and the plant looks good alongside irises, hostas or geraniums. Can be difficult when young. 30cm (12in) by 45cm (18in).

Dictamnus albus purpureus (Burning bush)

Upright deciduous. The common name comes from a flammable oil in the seed capsules which explodes when lit, without harming the plant – a novelty to impress visitors. The mauve-purple flowers are held on stately spikes in early to mid-summer. Plant with *Geranium psilostemon* and *Iris pallida*. 90cm (3ft) by 60cm (2ft).

Digitalis grandiflora (Perennial foxglove)

Upright evergreen. The common foxglove, *D. purpurea*, is a biennial, whereas this plant appears every year, producing its typical flower spikes in summer. The colour is creamy yellow. 60cm (2ft) by 30cm (12in).

Doronicum 'Miss Mason' (Leopard's bane)

Woofly deciduous. Doronicums all have bright yellow daisy-like flowers in spring and are easy to grow. This variety is one of the best, with comparatively short stems. 45cm (18in) by 60cm (2ft).

⌂ ❋ ❋ 🔲 ▦ C P ◧

Dryopteris filix-mas, D. affinis (Male fern, Buckler fern)

Woofly deciduous. Ferns are useful plants for shady spots in the garden, but most of them can be difficult to grow. These are not. They will grow and thrive almost anywhere, even coping with full sun. Grow with hostas and liriope. 90cm (3ft) (*filix-mas*) or 60cm (2ft) (*affinis*) by 60cm.

◖ ❋ ❋ ◧ 🔲 ▦ C P ◧

Epimedium perralderianum (Bishop's Hat)

Ball-shaped evergreen. Epimediums will grow under trees where little else will survive. This variety is the best for general use, as some of the others are rather small. The yellow flowers appear in early spring, but are hidden under the leaf canopy (some people cut the foliage away to reveal the flowers, but it is best grown for its foliage). 45cm (18in) by 30cm (12in).

◖ ❋ ❋ 🔲 C G ◧

Erodium pelargoniiflorum (Heron's bill)

Woofly evergreen. Most erodiums are miniature rock garden plants, but there are one or two larger ones which are perfect for the front of the border. This is one of them. Very similar to a hardy geranium, it has pale pink flowers for most of the summer. 30cm (12in) with a similar spread.

⌂ ❋ 🔲 ▦ C G ◧

Erysimum 'Bowles' Mauve' (Perennial wallflower)

Woofly evergreen. Wallflowers are well known as biennials and can look stunning when planted in association with tulips in amenity bedding schemes. The problem is that they have to be planted every year. This one is perennial. The foliage is grey and the purple flowers appear for a long period in the spring and summer. Grow with grey foliage shrubs. 60cm (2ft) by 45cm (18in).

◖ ❋ ❋ 🔲 M C

Euphorbia characias wulfenii (Wolf's milk)

Upright evergreen. Euphorbias come in a range of different shapes and sizes. Generally tough plants, they can become a nuisance in the wrong place. This one is perhaps the largest, with grey foliage topped by green flowers in early spring. Grow with large grasses and hydrangeas. 1.2m (4ft) by 90cm (3ft).

☑ ❋ ❋ ❋ 🔲 ▦ C M ◧

Euphorbia amygdaloides robbiae (Spurge, Rob's bonnet)

Horizontal evergreen. If planted in the wrong place, the invasive roots of this plant can be a nuisance. In harsh conditions under trees it is better-behaved. 60cm (2ft) with a similar spread.

◖ ❋ ❋ ❋ 🔲 ▦ C G ◧

Euphorbia myrsinites (Blue spurge)

Woofly evergreen. Often considered as a large rock garden plant, this euphorbia is quite useful at the front of a border, tumbling over a wall or across paving. Yellow flowers, appearing in spring. 15cm (6in) with a similar spread.

◖ ❋ 🔲 ▦ C M ◧

Geraniums (Cranesbills)

These hardy plants represent some of the very best herbaceous perennials available to the gardener. The name 'geranium' is frequently attached to the tender pelargoniums, used so much in summer bedding schemes and in containers. The range is enormous, but I have listed what I consider to be the best, working on the criteria of low maintenance and a long flowering season.

Geranium cinereum 'Ballerina'

Horizontal deciduous. Although considered an alpine, this plant is perfect for the front of a border, especially beside a path or patio. The veined pink flowers appear over a long period in the summer. 15cm (6in) with a similar spread.

◖ ❋ ❋ 🔲 ▦ C G ◧

Geranium macrorrhizum 'Ingwersen's Variety'.

Horizontal evergreen. This invasive geranium needs careful placing in the garden, as it can be a bully. Its evergreen foliage and pale pink flowers are useful, especially in harsh conditions under trees and shrubs. Grow with *Hosta sieboldiana* 'Elegans' and the fern *Dryopteris filix-mas*. 30cm (1ft) by 60cm (2ft).

☑ ❋ ❋ ❋ 🔲 ▦ C G ◧

Geranium psilostemon

Woofly deciduous. The finely cut foliage of this plant contrasts well with more solid shapes. The flowers are magenta pink. Grow in a scheme which includes delphiniums, roses and lavender. 1.2m (4ft) by 90cm (3ft).

⌂ ❋ ❋ 🔲 ▦ C P ◧

Soil

PH Must have an acid soil
Can cope with a light, dry sandy soil
C Grow well in clay soil
Will grow in any soil, but not damp
Will grow in damp or boggy conditions

Habit

G Good groundcover – the plant smothers the soil, stopping seeds from germinating.
M Some groundcover – the soil is covered but not enough to stop germination.
P Poor groundcover – there is a lot of bare soil around the plant.

Planting times

(these represent the optimum time of the year to plant – for more details see page 12)
Spring
Autumn
Summer

Geranium renardii

Woofly deciduous. Although this plant flowers early in the summer (usually May), the fine foliage persists to contribute to a planting scheme for most of the season. The flowers are blue-white and look good alongside *G. x rivearsleaianum* 'Russell Prichard'. 30cm (12in) with a similar spread.

Geranium x riversleaianum 'Russell Prichard'.

Horizontal deciduous. For such a small plant, this has one of the largest hearts. Its bright pink flowers appear in May and the display continues non-stop well into the autumn. Each plant spreads from a central rosette across a large area, but dies back to the central rosette at the end of the season. Grow with *G. renardii* or at the feet of *Rosa glauca*. 15 cm (6in) by 60cm (2ft).

Geranium x riversleaianum 'Mavis Simpson'.

Horizontal deciduous. This is the sister plant to 'Russell Prichard' and is identical apart from the flowers, which are a much paler pink.

Geranium sanguineum 'Striatum Splendens'

Horizontal deciduous. As with the *riversleaianum* varieties, this plant's pink flowers appear for most of the summer. Not to be confused with ordinary *G. sanguineum*, which is a much larger, coarser plant. Could also be labelled *G.s.* 'Lancastriense Splendens', 'Striatum' or 'Splendens' – the danger is that you might obtain the ordinary *G. sanguineum* by mistake. Grow along the front of a border consisting of *Iris germanica* and old roses. 15cm (6in) by 25cm (9in).

Geranium wallichianum 'Buxton's Variety'.

Horizontal deciduous. The leaves of this plant appear very late in the season and can be useful for hiding the foliage of earlier flowering plants like primulas or small spring bulbs. The flowers, which are held on the plant non-stop from the end of June right through, are a delightful blue, with white centres. 30cm (12in) by 60cm (2ft).

Gypsophila paniculata (Chalk plant)

When in flower this plant gives the impression of a white cloud hanging over the border. Gertrude Jekyll used it to solve the problem of oriental poppies, whose foliage collapses after flowering, leaving a gap in the border – she planted gypsophila behind them so that it would grow over the dying leaves. White flowers appear in July and August. 1m (3ft 3in) by up to 1.2m (4ft).

☑ ❋ ▨ ▤ C G (in flower)

Helictotrichon sempervirens (Oat grass)

Spiky evergreen. The pastel blue shade of this grass makes it an ideal choice for the front of the border and the scree bed. Plant it alongside *Hebe toparia*, *Nepeta nervosa* and bergenias for effect. 90cm (3ft) by 30cm (12in).

Helleborus argutifolius

Woofly evergreen. Often labelled as *H. lividus corsicus* or *H. corsicus*. This large architectural hellebore is useful as a contrast to small shrubs and large herbaceous perennials. It is best planted as a single specimen. 60cm (2ft) with a similar spread.

Helleborus orientalis (Lenten Rose)

Woofly evergreen. Most people are familiar with the Christmas Rose, *H. niger*, which has white bell-shaped flowers in December and January, but I have found this plant rather difficult to establish and have had much better success with the Lenten rose, which is similar but flowers later in the winter and early spring. It is also more variable in colour, producing flowers from plain white through to dark maroon with a variety of shades in between. 45cm (18in) by 60cm (2ft).

Helianthemum (Rock rose, Sun rose)

Horizontal evergreen. Generally considered to be a large alpine, the rock rose is perfect for the front of a hot sunny border, especially where it can tumble over a wall or paving. The flowers appear continually for most of the summer. 'Wisley Primrose' and 'Wisley Pink' are particularly good varieties with the bonus of grey foliage. Good reds are 'Red Orient' and 'Henfield Brilliant'. Rejuvenate by cutting back hard periodically. 15cm (6in) by 90cm (3ft).

Hemerocallis flava (Yellow day lily)

Spiky deciduous. Day lilies, so-called because each flower lasts only a day, are not just good for their flowers, but also for their grass-like foliage, which appears early in the year. Most of the flowers are yellow or orange, although there is a hard-to-obtain pink form and some brown ones. This one has pure

Key to codes

Availability
☑ **Easily obtainable. Should be available anywhere.**
◻ **May require some searching or could be seasonal, but should not be too difficult to find.**
⬛ **Best to order from a specialist nursery.**

Conditions **Sun or shade**
✳ **Shade**
✳ **Part shade**
✳ **Full sun**

yellow scented flowers in June, a month earlier than most of its relatives. Grow with blue geraniums. 70cm (2ft 3in) by 45cm (18in).

⬛✳✳◻▦▦C G◧

Hemerocallis 'Golden Chimes' (Day lily)
Spiky deciduous. Similar to *H. flava* but flowering a month later. 90cm (3ft) by 60cm (2ft).

☑✳✳◻▦▦C G◧

Hemerocallis 'Stella d'Oro' (Day lily)
Spiky deciduous. The previous two day lilies have been recommended for the variation in their flowering seasons, whereas this one is recommended because it is smaller in size. 45cm (18in) with a similar spread.

◻✳✳◻▦▦C G◧

Heuchera diversifolia 'Palace Purple' (Coral flower)
Woofly evergreen. There are a number of different heucheras available, most with luminescent pink flowers and small evergreen leaves. This one is very different – the foliage is much larger than the type and a rich wine purple. Makes a fine companion for bronze and variegated grasses and blue hostas. 45cm (18in) with a similar spread.

☑✳✳▦▦C M◧

Hostas (Plantain lilies)
Most hostas require shade and some damp in the soil, although I have found that the *sieboldiana* varieties are more tolerant and can even stand some sun. Many books describe the flowers of some hostas as being fragrant; the fact is that the temperature is rarely warm enough in the British Isles for the flowers to give off any scent. In America, where there is a great passion for the plants, the conditions are right and the full effect can be enjoyed. Perhaps the best way to enjoy the scent is to grow a scented variety in a cool conservatory.

The biggest enemies of the hosta are slugs and snails. Some hostas have large, ribbed leaves that are less palatable. Mulch around the plants with sharp grit and, if the problem persists, apply small amounts of slug chemical. The latter should be applied at regular intervals, starting in February, and covered with a tile or piece of wood to keep birds and animals away, not just from the chemical, but also from the dead bodies. If you don't want to use chemicals, make a trap using an old jam jar half filled with beer sunk into the ground; the offending

creatures will fall in and drown. Another organic approach is to lay some pieces of old carpet on the ground around the base of each plant – this will attract the slugs, which hide underneath during the day and can easily be dealt with. Slugs rarely travel far to feed so your solution should be applied locally.

Hosta fortunei albopicta
Large-leafed deciduous. The foliage of this plant is bright butter-yellow edged with pale green in the spring, darkening to two shades of green in the summer. 75cm (2ft 6in) by 60cm (2ft). *H. f. hyacinthina* has fine flowers and glaucous grey foliage.

◻✳✳▦C G◧

Hosta sieboldiana 'Elegans'
Large-leafed deciduous. This is one of the toughest hostas, even coping with full sun. It has large ribbed blue-grey leaves that are less palatable to slugs and snails and turn a butter-yellow in the autumn. 70cm (2ft 3in) by 60cm (2ft).

☑✳✳◻▦C G◧

Hosta sieboldiana 'Frances Williams'
Large-leafed deciduous. Looks the same as 'Elegans' but with a yellow edge to the leaves.

◻✳✳◻▦C G◧

✿ *Hosta sieboldiana* **'Elegans' and** *Polystichum setiferum.*

Hosta 'Halcyon'
Large-leafed deciduous. The foliage of this plant is a gunmetal blue, which can appear very blue in humid conditions, perhaps near a pool of water. Grow it alongside

H. 'Thomas Hogg' and in front of rodgersias for a fine cooling effect. 45cm (18in) by 30cm (12in).

Hosta 'Thomas Hogg'

Large-leafed deciduous. Many hostas have white variegation, and this is one of the easiest to find. It has white margins to the leaves, contrasting well with 'Halycon'. 60cm (2ft) by 45cm (18in).

Hosta 'Sum and Substance'

Large-leafed deciduous. Sometimes a hosta with very large leaves is useful as a 'full-stop' plant. It has very large ribbed apple-green foliage and is said to be better grown in full sun, where the foliage will be more of a golden-green. 90cm (3ft) by 75cm (2ft 6in).

Iberis 'Snowflake' (Candytuft)

Horizontal evergreen. Considered to be a large alpine, this low evergreen is perfect for the edge of a border, especially trailing across paving or over a wall. The flowers are white and appear from April to June. 25cm (9in) by 60cm (2ft).

Iris foetidissima 'Variegata' (Gladwyn iris)

Spiky evergreen. This is the queen of foliage irises. Unlike its plain green cousin, it is refined and generally healthy-looking, even after a hard winter. Sadly, it is difficult to propagate and can be difficult to find, but is well worth searching for. The flowers, if produced at all, are lilac in colour and insignificantly small. 60cm (2ft) by 45cm (18in).

Iris 'Blue Denim'

Spiky deciduous. Bearded irises in flower are one of the highlights of the garden in spring, but they can be quite large in both height and spread. There are certain instances where that size is not desirable and a smaller version is required. There are many available, but I have found this variety comparatively easy to obtain. 30cm (1ft) with a similar spread.

Iris germanica (Bearded iris)

Spiky deciduous. Mention the word 'iris' and it is invariably the tall bearded *I. germanica* that comes into everybody's mind. The displays in May and June are nothing short of magnificent; the colours are purples, lilacs, whites, blues, yellows, oranges, depending on the variety, and some are even scented. They associate well with roses, geraniums, lavender and delphiniums; try planting sweet violets, *Viola odorata*, or *V. labradorica* between them. Up to 90cm (3ft) with a similar spread.

Iris kampfaeri (Japanese iris)

Spiky deciduous. Water and bog garden plants can be a serious problem; many are aggressive and invasive, which is why they are normally planted in baskets at the pool's edge. This water iris is comparatively well-behaved and brings some welcome colour to the garden in summer. The flower colour is either white or a shade of purple or pink, depending upon the variety. Usually grown at the water's edge, or in wet soil, it can be grown in a normal border as long as the soil is acid or neutral with plenty of rich humus incorporated. 70cm (2ft 3in) by 45cm (18in).

Iris pallida 'Variegata'

Spiky deciduous. Similar to *I. foetidissima* 'Variegata', but the green in the foliage has more of a blue tinge. It is also deciduous. However, it is easier to propagate and therefore easier to find, and its sweetly scented, lavender-blue flowers are pleasing. 70cm (2ft 3in) by 30cm (1ft).

Iris pseudoacorus (Common yellow flag)

Spiky deciduous. This common native waterside plant normally grows in damp soil close to water, but readily seeds itself in drier soils. The most difficult gardening conditions are where there is a rising and falling water-table or a river which floods, and the yellow flag copes admirably in these conditions. Having said this I would not plant it as a matter of course, but only where conditions demand it – a kind of trouble-shooter plant. The yellow flowers are held on tall stems in early summer. 1.2m (4ft) with a similar spread.

(only shade in damp soil)

Iris unguicularis (Algerian iris)

Spiky evergreen. Winter-flowering plants are always worth having in the garden and this one is no exception. It flowers from autumn through to spring as long as it has the right conditions – poor soil in full sun at the base of a wall. Once established, it must be left undisturbed. The problem is that the flowers are held low down in the centre of the leaf rosette and can easily be missed. 45cm (18in) by 30cm (1ft).

Key to codes

Availability
☑ Easily obtainable. Should be available anywhere.
◖ May require some searching or could be seasonal, but should not be too difficult to find.
⌂ Best to order from a specialist nursery.

Conditions **Sun or shade**
✳ **Shade**
✳ **Part shade**
✳ **Full sun**

Kniphofia 'Little Maid'
Spiky evergreen. The common name, 'red hot poker', gives a false impression of this superb garden plant. The flowers are small 'pokers' of a pleasing yellow in late summer and autumn. Combine this with evergreen grass-like foliage on an accommodating plant and its charms can easily be seen. 45cm (18in) with a similar spread.

Kniphofia uvaria (Red Hot Poker)
Spiky evergreen. The red hot poker is perhaps one of the few garden plants which most people can recognize. It can, however, be extremely difficult to find a particular named variety, this being one of the easiest. The typical red and yellow pokers are held on tall stems in late summer and autumn above solid spiky leaf rosettes. Although an herbaceous perennial, it has the size and stature of a shrub and is useful as a structural plant in the border. Up to 1.5m (5ft) by 60cm (2ft). *K.* 'Atlanta' (early summer flowering) and *K.* 'Royal Standard' (summer) are similar.

Libertia grandiflora (New Zealand Satin Flower)
Spiky evergreen. Although considered to require sun and a protected site, I have found this plant happy in shade as long as it is snuggled by surrounding plants or protected by a fence or wall. It has white flowers on long spikes in summer over grass-like foliage and can produce orange seed heads in autumn, so beware of a colour clash at this time. 60cm (2ft) with a similar spread.

Ligularia przewalskii
Upright deciduous. This has attractive deeply-fingered dark green leaves with nearly black stems. The flowers, which appear in mid-summer, are yellow, held on tall spires. 1.8m (6ft) by 90cm (3ft). *L.* 'The Rocket' is similar.

Liriope muscari (Big blue lily turf)
Spiky evergreen. One of the gems of the garden, this will grow happily in dry shade (and tolerates full sun), where its 'grape hyacinth' blue flowers appear every autumn. Grow with colchicums and/or *Nerine bowdenii*. 30cm (12in) by 45cm (18in). *L. muscari* 'Monroe White' has white flowers.

Lithospermum diffusum 'Heavenly Blue'
Horizontal evergreen. This delightful ground-hugging plant has bright blue flowers in early summer and occasional ones through the rest of the growing season. It needs the warmth of a patio and is ideal around the base of a pergola. One drawback is that it needs a lime-free soil, but this can be supplied by planting it in ericaceous compost, as the roots are fairly shallow. 10cm (4in) by 60cm (2ft).

Miscanthus sinensis 'Gracillimus' (Chinese silver grass)
Spiky evergreen. Grasses have been under-used in the garden for many years, due mainly to a fear of them becoming invasive. This stately plant should put everyone's mind at rest. It has long arching, graceful leaves which in themselves can reach 1.5m (5ft) in length. The whole effect contrasts well with the more solid shape of hydrangeas. 1.5m (5ft) by 1.2m (4ft).

Milium effusum 'Aureum' (Bowles' golden grass)
Spiky deciduous. Every part of this plant is bright yellow. However, it must be planted in light shade to maintain this colouring or it will turn green. Plant with *Viola labradorica*. 30cm (12in) by 20cm (8in).

Monarda didyma 'Cambridge Scarlet' (Bee balm)
Most herbs do not make particularly good garden plants, but this is an exception. As a herb, the leaves can be steeped in boiling water to make a refreshing drink; as a garden plant it has large plum-scarlet flowers in high summer. 90cm (3ft) by 45cm (18in).

Nepeta nervosa (Catmint)
Horizontal evergreen. Plants which flower at the front of the border for many weeks are a boon, and this plant fits that bill. The blue flowers appear first in May, and, with periodic dead-heading, repeat throughout the summer. With luck, it will still be flowering in the autumn. Grow with lavender and *Geranium* 'Russell Prichard'. 30cm (12in) by 45cm (18in).

Nepeta mussinii (Catmint)
Upright evergreen. This has the same characteristics as *N. nervosa* but it is much taller. 45cm (18in) with a similar spread.

creative gardening for busy people

Soil
PH **Must have an acid soil**
Can cope with a light, dry sandy soil
C **Grow well in clay soil**
Will grow in any soil, but not damp
Will grow in damp or boggy conditions

Habit
G **Good groundcover** –the plant smothers the soil, stopping seeds from germinating.
M **Some groundcover** – the soil is covered but not enough to stop germination.
P **Poor groundcover** – there is a lot of bare soil around the plant.

Planting times
(these represent the optimum time of the year to plant – for more details see page 12)
Spring
Autumn
Summer

Ophiopogon planiscapus 'Nigrescens'
Spiky evergreen. This curious plant has grass-like foliage which is almost black. Although it will grow at the front of a border, it is best grown in a scree bed where the foliage will stand out better against the background. 20cm (8in) with a similar spread.

Osteospermums (African Daisy)
Horizontal evergreen. The advantage of these plants is that they will flower from May through to the first frosts. The disadvantage is that many of the hybrids are not hardy enough to negotiate the British winter. The warm winter weather throughout the 1990s has meant that many are now surviving. *O. jucundum* is probably the hardiest; if planted in full sun it will form a spreading mat, so is best near plants which can look after themselves. 45cm (18in) by 60cm (2ft).

Paeonia 'Felix Crousse' (Peony)
Woofly deciduous. There is little to compare with peonies for late spring colour. The large deep red, ball-shaped blooms of this variety are a precursor to the joys of the summer, and the foliage continues to look good long after the flowers have faded. Once the clumps have developed, it is best left alone; if moved, or split up, plants tend to sulk for a number of years before flowering again. Up to 90cm (3ft) by 60cm (2ft).

Paeonia 'Sarah Bernhardt' (Peony)
Woofly deciduous. A pink version of the above.

Platycodon grandiflorus mariesii (Balloon flower)
Woofly deciduous. This unusual plant has wide blue cup-shaped flowers opening from balloon shaped buds appearing in late summer. 60cm (2ft) by 45cm (18in).

Polygonatum × hybridum (Solomon's seal)
Weeping deciduous. Tiny bells of creamy white flowers appear in clusters along arching stems in April and May. Looks good growing with hostas. 30cm (12in) by 90cm (3ft).

Polygonum affine 'Donald Lowndes' (Knotweed)
Upright deciduous. Not all knotweeds are good for the garden, in fact many can be a serious, invasive nuisance, especially in damp soil. This one one is less so but still needs to be planted with confident neighbours. It has a long flowering season which starts in midsummer and continues into the autumn. The flowers are pink and held on short upright spikes. 30cm (12in) with a similar spread.

Polystichum setiferum (Soft shield fern)
Woofly evergreen. This fern is one of the most tolerant, coping with dry or damp conditions in shade or part shade. Looks good with hostas or grape vines. 1.2m (4ft) by 90cm (3ft).

Primula vulgaris (Primrose)
Horizontal deciduous. The primrose, native to the British Isles, makes a fine front of the border plant and is ideal naturalized in grass or woodland. The small yellow flowers are produced in March and April above a crinkle-leafed rosette of fresh green leaves. 10cm (4in) by 30cm (12in).

Rheum palmatum (Ornamental rhubarb)
Large-leafed deciduous. This bog garden plant should be the first choice in this type of garden if there is sufficient space. Looks stately when growing over the edge of open water. I have seen it growing in ordinary dry soil. 1.2m (4ft) with a similar spread.

Rodgersia aesculifolia, R. pinnata 'Elegans'
Another bog garden plant, but one which will cope with ordinary soil as long as it is not too dry. In damp conditions it can be a robust invader, but in ordinary soil it remains fairly static. Grow with *Hosta* 'Halcyon'. 90cm (3ft) by 60cm (2ft). (shade or part-shade when not grown in a damp soil).

Salvia nemerosa 'East Friesland'
Woofly deciduous. There are a number of herbaceous salvias which provide brilliant splashes of colour in midsummer. Many, however, are not reliably hardy. This one, with rich royal blue flowers on medium height spikes, is one of the hardiest and also the easiest to find. The matt olive-green foliage is a fine foil for grasses and horizontal plants. 70cm (2ft 3in) by 45cm (18in).

Saxifraga × urbium (London pride)
Horizontal evergreen. Most saxifragas are cushion-forming

123

Key to codes

Availability
☑ **Easily obtainable. Should be available anywhere.**
🔎 **May require some searching or could be seasonal, but should not be too difficult to find.**
🏠 **Best to order from a specialist nursery.**

Conditions Sun or shade
❋ **Shade**
❋ **Part shade**
❋ **Full sun**

alpine plants, some being among the tiniest available, but this plant is much larger, making it ideal for the front of a border. Tiny pink flowers are held profusely on short stalks in early to mid-summer. 25cm (9in) with a similar spread.

☑ ❋ ❋ ❋ ▦ ▦ C G ◀

Sedum spectabile 'Autumn Joy' (Ice plant)

Woofly deciduous. Nearly every garden has at least one clump of the ice plant – it is very accommodating, growing almost anywhere, although it is better in full sun. The flowers are tiny, held on flat circular flower heads in late summer, and are much loved by butterflies. The foliage is glaucous and succulent, and makes a good companion for caryopteris or ceratostigma.
60cm (2ft) by 45cm (18in).

☑ ❋ ❋ ❋ ▦ ▦ C M ◀

Sedum 'Ruby Glow'

Woofly deciduous. This sedum has bluish-green foliage which trails across the ground, and deep mauve-pink flowers in the autumn. Good for the front of a border or in a scree bed.
20cm (8in) by 15cm (6in).

🔎 ❋ ▦ ▦ C P ◀

Sisyrinchium striatum (Satin flower)

Spiky evergreen. Small creamy-yellow daisy-like flowers are held on tall spikes in mid- to late summer. The clumps develop quickly and the display is quite spectacular. It can be a little invasive, seeding itself readily. Cut off any dead leaves when they appear. 70cm (2ft 3in) by 60cm (2ft).

☑ ❋ ❋ ❋ ▦ ▦ C M ◀

Stipa gigantea (Golden oats)

Spiky evergreen. This large grass makes a spectacular display in mid- to late summer with its tall flowers, similar to a miniature pampas grass. Up to 1.8m (6ft) by 90cm (3ft).

🔎 ❋ ❋ ❋ ▦ ▦ C G ◀

Valeriana officinalis (Valerian)

Upright deciduous. This plant loves to grow at the feet of walls and in paving, where it can become a nuisance, seeding itself around with its roots difficult to extract. Despite this, the display can be spectacular and anyone who loves it will forgive it anything. The flower spikes range in colour from white, through different shades of red, pink and purple, appearing for long periods in the height of the summer. 1.2m (4ft) by 90cm (3ft).

☑ ❋ ❋ ❋ ▦ ▦ C M ◀

Viola labradorica

Horizontal evergreen. The purplish green foliage and lavender-blue violet flowers of this plant are a welcome sign that spring is just around the corner. Grow among *Iris germanica*.
10cm (4in) by 30cm (1ft).

🔎 ❋ ❋ ❋ ❋ ▦ ▦ C G ◀

Zantedeschia aethiopica (Arum lily)

Large-leafed deciduous. The magnificent white flowers of this plant are almost unreal, looking as if they have been composed of the finest white china. It prefers a damp soil, but will grow quite happily in ordinary soil which is not too dry.
60cm (2ft) with a similar spread.

🔎 ❋ ❋ ◑ ▦ C M ◀

✿ *Stipa gigantea.*

Shrubs

The definition of a shrub is a plant where several woody stems arise from the surface of the soil. This is a very rough definition and I can think of a number of plants which do not match this description but are generally thought of a shrubs (yuccas, for instance).

Shrubs are generally low in maintenance, but they can be a little short of colour and, in a small to medium garden, need herbaceous perennials at their base to complete the scene. They are important for screening, both from view and from noise, the large-leafed shrubs being best for muffling sound. They form the framework, the structure, or the palette of a garden against which the gardener splashes his more colourful plants.

Soil
- **PH** Must have an acid soil
- Can cope with a light, dry sandy soil
- **C** Grow well in clay soil
- Will grow in any soil, but not damp
- Will grow in damp or boggy conditions

Habit
- **G** Good groundcover – the plant smothers the soil, stopping seeds from germinating.
- **M** Some groundcover – the soil is covered but not enough to stop germination.
- **P** Poor groundcover – there is a lot of bare soil around the plant.

Planting times
(these represent the optimum time of the year to plant – for more details see page 12)
- Spring
- Autumn
- Summer

Top 100 shrubs

Abelia × grandiflora
Ball-shaped semi-evergreen. The scented flowers of this plant are a welcome addition to the garden in late summer. 1.2m (4ft) with a similar spread.

Acer palmatum 'Dissectum' (Japanese maple)
Woofly deciduous shrub. These diminutive trees form a feathery mound which is a fine companion to many plants. Although they prefer acidity, they are quite happy in alkaline soil. They must have protection from cold wind, which could kill them. Good for growing in a medium-sized container. 1.2m (4ft) with a similar spread.

Amelanchier lamarkii (Snowy mespilus)
Ball-shaped deciduous. This plant has so much going for it. It has a brilliant display of small star shaped white flowers from mid- to late spring, and brilliant red and orange foliage in autumn. Can be trained as a tree. 2m (6ft 6in) by 2.4m (8ft).

Arbutus unedo (Strawberry tree)
Ball-shaped evergreen. Although purported to be on the tender side, it grows very successfully in the heavy clay soil around Bedford. Its common name comes from the strawberry-like fruit. It will eventually form a medium-sized tree, but in its younger years makes a solid ball with a nice 'skirt' to ground level. 1.5m (5ft) with a similar spread.

Artemisia 'Powys Castle'
Woofly evergreen. A wonderful addition to the traditional border, where it combines well with roses and herbaceous plants. Cut it down to the ground each spring or it will become untidy and straggly. From this rough treatment it will grow up to 1.2m (4 ft) in diameter by the autumn, smothering its unfortunate neighbours as it goes. Allow it 1–1.2m and lightly trim in late summer to keep it under control. 60–80 cm (2ft-2ft 6in) in height.

Aucuba japonica 'Variegata' (Spotted laurel)
Ball-shaped evergreen. This common plant is useful in very difficult conditions, even growing under trees. It is a great companion for yellow flowers and I like to grow it with *Rosa* 'Graham Thomas'. It will grow anywhere, but should be saved for those difficult spots . Top prune to encourage 'skirt'. 1.2 m (4ft) with a similar spread.

Berberis (Barberry)
There are many different berberis, both evergreen and deciduous, but many can be hard to find. Most are best used in large landscaping applications and should not be planted in the private garden. They have small orange flowers in spring which can sometimes ruin a planting scheme as they do not combine well with other colours. They are all covered in thorns, making them a useful deterrent, *B. julianae*, with larger than average spines, being the best for this. Those listed below have characteristics which can be of use in the private garden.

Berberis buxifolia 'Nana'
Ball-shaped evergreen. As the Latin name suggests, this plant resembles box (*Buxus sempervirens*). Useful at the front of the border it makes a fine structural plant, providing balance and marking key points. 60cm (2ft) with a similar spread.

❀ *Aucuba japonica* **makes a fine companion for** *Rosa* **'Graham Thomas'**

Berberis candidula 'Amstelveen'
Weeping evergreen. This small berberis has a useful shape for completing a planting scheme. The leaves are blue-green with a powder blue underside, creating an interesting effect. 80cm (2ft 6in) with a similar spread.

Availability

☑ **Easily obtainable. Should be available anywhere.**

🔎 **May require some searching or could be seasonal, but should not be too difficult to find.**

🏠 **Best to order from a specialist nursery.**

Conditions **Sun or shade**

❋ **Shade**

❋ **Part shade**

❋ **Full sun**

Berberis thunbergii 'Atropurpurea nana'

Ball-shaped deciduous. A small purple-leafed shrub, ideal for contrasting with yellows. Try growing it in a circle around the feet of *Thuja* 'Rheingold'. 50cm (1ft 8in) with a similar spread.

☑ ❋ ❋ 🌿 💧 ▦ C M ◐ ◑

Berberis thunbergii 'Kobold'

Ball-shaped deciduous. A green version of *B. t.* 'Atropurpurea Nana'.

☑ ❋ ❋ ❋ 💧 ▦ C M ◐ ◑

Berberis verruculosa

Weeping evergreen. A useful structural plant which will grow a little larger than the other recommended berberis. 1.2m (4ft) with a similar spread.

🔎 ❋ ❋ ❋ 💧 ▦ C G M ◑

Buddleia davidii 'Black Knight' (Butterfly bush)

Woofly deciduous. There are many different varieties of buddleia, the colour of the flowers varying from white through to the very dark purple of 'Black Knight'. There is also a yellow one. Prune to the ground every spring to produce a more floriferous display. Despite the harsh treatment it will reach 1.5–2m (5–6ft 6in) by 1.8m (6ft).

☑ ❋ ❋ 💧 ▦ C P ◐ ◑

Buddleia davidii 'Nano Blue' (Butterfly bush)

Woofly deciduous. This has been included because of its smaller size. Even then it grows to 1.5m (5ft) with a similar spread. The flowers are royal blue. Treat as 'Black Knight'.

🔎 ❋ ❋ ❋ 💧 ▦ C P ◐ ◑

Buddleia x 'Lochinch' (Butterfly bush)

Woofly deciduous. This buddleia has the same dimensions as 'Black Knight' but the foliage is grey-green, creating a different effect. The flowers are powdery blue. Treat as 'Black Knight'.

🔎 ❋ ❋ ❋ 💧 ▦ C P ◐ ◑

Buxus sempervirens (Box)

Ball-shaped . A native of the British Isles, this plant will grow almost anywhere and has been used for centuries in formal displays. It is an ideal choice for use in topiary and can be clipped to almost any shape. Can be clipped to maintain a smaller size and grown as a hedge. 1.2m (4ft) with a similar spread.

☑ ❋ ❋ ❋ 💧 ▦ C ◐ ◑

Buxus sempervirens 'Eligantissimum' (Box)

Ball-shaped evergreen. This is a box with creamy variegated foliage and is slower growing than the plain green version. All other details as green box.

🔎 ❋ ❋ ❋ 💧 ▦ C G ◐ ◑

Buxus sempervirens 'Suffruticosa' (Edging box)

Ball-shaped evergreen. This is a true miniature and is used to create the tiny step-over hedging much seen edging borders and paths. Very slow growing. 20cm (8in) with a similar spread.

🏠 ❋ ❋ ❋ 💧 ▦ C G ◐ ◑

Camellia 'Donation'

Ball-shaped evergreen. Camellias are often thought of as difficult, needing special conditions. True, they prefer acid soil and they must be protected from the rising sun, which will damage the blooms on frosty spring mornings, but otherwise they are reasonably easy. Their magnificent display is more than enough reward for this extra trouble. They will grow on alkaline soil but need a sheltered north- or west-facing spot that is screened from the east and has plenty of organic matter dug in. This variety has pink flowers. 1.8m (6ft) with a similar spread. 'Anticipation' is similar but with red flowers.

🔎 ❋ ❋ ❋ C G ◑

Carpenteria californicum

Ball-shaped evergreen. Fairly upright in growth for a ball shape, this plant requires a south-facing protected site, preferably against a wall. In the warmer counties it can be grown in a more open site. The magnificent display of white flowers appears in mid-summer. 1.5m (5ft) with a similar spread.

🏠 ❋ 💧 ▦ C M ◑

Caryopteris x clandonensis 'Heavenly Blue' (Blue beard)

Woofly deciduous. The shape is difficult to define exactly, each stem being fairly upright, but the foliage is an attractive grey-green which determined the definition. Apart from this, it is best described as a miniature buddleia, with blue flowers in late summer much loved by butterflies. 1m (3ft 3in) with a similar spread. Grow with rosemary, agapanthus or *Sedum spectabile*.

☑ ❋ ❋ ❋ 💧 ▦ C P ◑

Ceratostigma willmottianum (Shrubby plumbago)

Woofly deciduous. The bright, almost luminous, blue of this plant's flowers are always eye-catching in late summer and early autumn. Cut hard back in April. Looks good with fuchsias and

Soil
- PH Must have an acid soil
- Can cope with a light, dry sandy soil
- C Grow well in clay soil
- Will grow in any soil, but not damp
- Will grow in damp or boggy conditions

Habit
- G Good groundcover –the plant smothers the soil, stopping seeds from germinating.
- M Some groundcover – the soil is covered but not enough to stop germination.
- P Poor groundcover – there is a lot of bare soil around the plant.

Planting times
(these represent the optimum time of the year to plant – for more details see page 12)
- Spring
- Autumn
- Summer

Sedum spectabile. 80cm (2ft 6in) by 60cm (2ft).

Choisya ternata (Mexican orange blossom)
Ball-shaped evergreen. This easy to grow shrub has scented white flowers in May and again in October. Good at the back of a traditional rose and herbaceous border. 1.8m (6ft) by 2m (6ft 6in).

Choisya 'Aztec Pearl'
Woofly evergreen. A comparatively recent development, this is a similar plant to *C. ternata* but with more finely divided feathery foliage. 1.5 m (5ft) with a similar spread.

Clerodendrum trichotomum (Glory tree)
Woofly deciduous. Covered in small white and maroon scented flowers this is one of the top plants for a late summer display. 2m (6ft 6in) with a similar spread.

Convulvulus cneorum
Woofly evergreen. Related to bindweed, this small silver-leafed plant has white funnel-shaped flowers in June and July. Excellent on a hot sunny patio where it can flop over the edge of the paving. 80cm (2ft 6in) with a similar spread.

Cordyline australis (Cabbage palm)
Spiky evergreen. This palm is not generally thought of as being hardy, but in recent years it has come through the winter quite successfully in Bedfordshire – even in exposed sites. Despite this, care should be taken in siting it and even some thought given to applying winter protection (best done by pulling all the leaves together into a spike and covering with raffia paper). Although it will flower when mature, it is grown for the shape of its foliage which will drop off as it grows, forming a palm-like trunk. Great for adding impact to a group, especially a group of containers. 1.2m (4ft) by 1m (3ft 3in).

Cornus alba 'Elegantissimum' (Dogwood)
Woofly deciduous. Famed for its red winter stems, this is the best of the dogwoods, with its variegated leaves. Can be treated in one of two ways: pruned hard in April to encourage brighter stems and keep the plant small, or unpruned, to maintain a large rambling plant. Looks good next to water either way. 1.5m (5ft) by 1.2m

(4ft) – pruned. 2.5m (8ft 3in) with a similar spread – unpruned.

(pruned) G (unpruned)

Cotinus coggygria 'Grace' (Smoke bush)
Woofly deciduous. The common name refers to the effect created by the flowers on the original plant, but this variety is grown for its purple foliage. The foliage makes a good backdrop for many colours, contrasting with yellows, whites and oranges, and intensifying pinks and blues. Can be pruned annually to create a smaller plant with much larger foliage. A good 'skirt' is created if the plant is left unpruned and the base opened to the sun. 1.8m (6ft) by 1.5m (5ft) – unpruned. 1.2 m (4ft) with a similar spread – pruned.

G (unpruned)

Danaë racemosa (Alexandrian laurel)
Weeping evergreen. This is a small, tough, shade-loving evergreen, much sought after by flower arrangers. 80cm (2ft 6in) with a similar spread.

Daphne mezereum (Mezereon)
Woofly deciduous. Although this plant looses its leaves in the winter, its purple flowers appear in January and February on bare stems. The problem is that it can be very expensive and temperamental (watering with sequestered iron early in its life appears to settle it in). Hates being pruned. The only alternative I have found, is *Viburnum farreri* 'Nanum', which flowers on bare stems and is the same size and shape, but can be more difficult to find. 80 cm (2ft 6in) with a similar spread.

Elaeagnus × *ebbingei, E.* × *e.* 'Limelight'
Woofly evergreen. Can be trimmed to form a ball, or even trained as a hedge. The plain green variety has grey undersides to the leaves, giving the whole plant a steel-grey appearance, and it is one of the fastest-growing evergreens and useful where some quick screening is required. 'Limelight' has green and yellow variegated foliage (any branches with plain green leaves should be removed). 2m (6ft 6in) with a similar spread (the plain-coloured variety will reach these sizes faster). A similar green and yellow variegated variety is *E. pungens* 'Maculata', which is smaller-growing than 'Limelight' (1.8m (6ft) with a similar spread).

Key to codes

Availability
☑ Easily obtainable. Should be available anywhere.
◎ May require some searching or could be seasonal, but should not be too difficult to find.
⌂ Best to order from a specialist nursery.

Conditions Sun or shade
✳ Shade
✳ Part shade
✳ Full sun

Euonymus europaeus 'Red Cascade' (Spindle tree)
Woofly deciduous. This is the ornamental version of a native hedgerow plant (*E. alata*). Its attraction comes in the autumn when the leaves turn a brilliant orange-red and are accompanied by curious three-sided red fruits. 1.5m (5ft) with a similar spread.

◎ ✳ ✳ ✳ ▣ ▦ ▣ C P ◪ ◨

Euonymus fortunei 'Silver Queen'
(Evergreen bittersweet)
Ball-shaped evergreen. It is difficult to decide upon the shape of this plant, as it tends to throw out horizontal branches, but it will respond to pruning so I have included it under 'ball-shaped'. There appears to be some confusion in the industry between the varieties 'Emerald Gaiety', 'Silver Queen' and 'Variegata', in fact I am not 100 per cent certain which is which. They all have green and white variegated leaves and have the ability to climb walls, where they attach themselves using rootlets on the underside of the branches. 80cm (2ft 6in) by 90cm (3ft).

☑ ✳ ✳ ✳ ▣ ▦ ▣ C G ◪ ◨

Euonymus fortunei 'Emerald 'n' Gold'
(Evergreen bittersweet)
Ball-shaped evergreen. This is similar to 'Silver Queen' but with green and yellow foliage.

☑ ✳ ✳ ✳ ▣ ▦ ▣ C G ◪ ◨

Exochorda × macrantha 'The Bride' (Pearl bush)
Weeping deciduous. Although flowering for such a short time in the late spring/early summer, the spectacular display of falling white blooms is well worth finding space for. It also looks good when trained as a standard. 2m (2ft 6in) by 1.8m (6ft). If left unpruned it will form a 'skirt'.

◎ ✳ ✳ ✳ ▦ ▣ C M ◪ ◨

Fargesia murieliae (Bamboo)
Upright evergreen. Bamboos have a reputation for being invasive, but this is a little unfair. True, some can be a severe problem, but this one, which forms a solid clump, is not one of those. (Although the Royal Horticultural Society suggest that its spread is infinite, I can only imagine that this is over a very long period, in absolutely perfect conditions.) Grow with architectural shapes like fatsia or *Mahonia japonica*. 2 metres (6ft 6in) with a similar spread (this can vary dramatically depending upon the conditions). *F. nitida* is similar, but with black stems.

☑ ✳ ✳ ✳ ▣ ▦ ▣ C M ◪ ◨

Fatsia japonica (Castor oil plant)
Woofly evergreen. An excellent large evergreen, often confused with more tender houseplants. Preferring a shady spot, it has a tremendous capacity for coping with dry shade under trees. Its large palmate leaves, the largest of any hardy evergreen, are an excellent foil for less architectural shapes. Grow with bamboos. 1.5m (5ft) with a similar spread

☑ ✳ ✳ ▣ ▦ ▣ C M ◪ ◨

Fuchsia 'Mrs Popple'
Weeping deciduous. Although it does not start to flower until well into the summer, this small shrub flowers for 4–5 months. The flowers are unusually large for a hardy fuchsia, which has led to some confusion with its tender cousins. Reputed to need full sunlight, it is happier with some respite from the full heat of the sun and will grow near a north-facing wall or fence. The plant will die down every year to ground level from where it will throw up new shoots in the spring, so cut back the previous year's growth in early spring. This tendency to die back in the spring means that any 'skirting' is only effective from midsummer onwards. Try growing with variegated hostas and *Hebe toparia*. 80cm (2ft 6in) with a similar spread.

☑ ✳ ✳ ▣ ▦ ▣ C M ◨

Genista lydia
Weeping deciduous. This plant, related to broom and gorse, benefits from the best qualities of both. The wiry branches cascade out from the centre of the plant and, although deciduous, the green branches maintain a presence through the winter. Pea-like yellow flowers in late spring/early summer. 60cm (2ft) by 80cm (2ft 6in).

☑ ✳ ▣ ▦ ▣ C M ◪ ◨

Hebes

There are a vast number of these evergreen garden gems in cultivation. They will flower over a long period in summer and, being evergreen, provide colour all the year round. Their main drawback is that they can be tender, especially the large-leafed varieties, which should only be planted in a sheltered spot with a lot of protection. It is not so much the cold that is the problem, but any accompanying wind, usually from the east or north. Never plant a hebe in the autumn, as they need a summer's growth before facing their first winter. They hybridize very readily and new ones are constantly coming on the market – these new varieties have no track record and it is difficult to know how they will develop. The following are ones

creative gardening for busy people

Soil
PH Must have an acid soil
S Can cope with a light, dry sandy soil
C Grow well in clay soil
S Will grow in any soil, but not damp
D Will grow in damp or boggy conditions

Habit
G Good groundcover –the plant smothers the soil, stopping seeds from germinating.
M Some groundcover – the soil is covered but not enough to stop germination.
P Poor groundcover – there is a lot of bare soil around the plant.

Planting times
(these represent the optimum time of the year to plant – for more details see page 12)
D Spring
   Autumn
※ Summer

that I use on a regular basis and have found to be reliable:

Hebe 'Autumn Glory'

Ball-shaped evergreen. A medium-sized hebe with a more upright growing habit. It carries purple flower spikes from mid-summer to early winter. Not 100 per cent hardy and requires a protected site. 1.2m (4ft) by 1m (may grow larger in near perfect conditions). If in full sun and top pruned it will develop a 'skirt'.

Hebe 'Carl Teschner'.

Horizontal evergreen. A ground-hugging shrub, with purplish blue flowers in summer. Grow on the edge of a path, patio or in a gravelled area. Very hardy. Good ground cover generally, although if not happy it will open up, allowing gaps to appear. 15cm (6in) by 80cm (2ft 6in).

Hebe 'Great Orme'

Ball-shaped evergreen. Small shrub with flowers in pink spikes from mid-summer to early winter. Although the leaves are not small, I have found this shrub to be reasonably hardy; however, avoid exposure to north and east winds. Fairly open in habit but it will 'skirt' if conditions are to its liking and it is left unpruned. 80cm (2ft 6in) with a similar spread (1.5m in height in perfect conditions).

Hebe 'Mrs Winder'

Ball-shaped evergreen. Another small shrub, this time with purplish-bronze leaves. It has blue flowers in summer but is grown mainly for the foliage effect. 80cm (2ft 6in) by 70cm (2ft 3in).

Hebe rakaiensis

Ball-shaped evergreen. Plain green. Forms a smothering dome requiring no trimming to maintain its shape. Good to mark key points like path corners, as a low-maintenance alternative to box (*Buxus sempervirens*). Dense spikes of white flowers in summer. 80cm (2ft 6in) with a similar spread.

Hebe toparia

Ball-shaped evergreen. Small grey leaves, for a sunny position. Grows reliably into a small ground-covering dome which is perfect for disguising the edges of paving. It has small leaves, which makes it fairly hardy, but nevertheless some care should be taken in colder areas. Dense spikes of white flowers in summer. 60cm (2 ft) with a similar spread. Try growing with *Abelia x grandiflora*.

Hydrangea macrophylla 'Mariesii'

Ball-shaped deciduous. Generally the most common hydrangeas can be split into two groups: the mop-head, or hortensis, varieties and the lacecap varieties. The mop-head can look a little artificial and is a personal taste, whereas the lacecap flowers are much more refined and fit in better with mixed planting schemes. Although hydrangeas prefer a rich leafy soil, they will grow in almost anything. Up to 1.5m (5ft) by 1.2m. Try growing alongside *Miscanthus sinensis* 'Gracillimus'.

Hypericum 'Hidcote' (St John's wort)

Ball-shaped evergreen. Hypericums, in general, are not good garden plants, but this one is an exception. Its yellow flowers appear from mid-summer onwards, giving a good long season. 1.8m (6ft) by 1.8m.

Kerria japonica 'Variegata' (Bachelor's buttons)

Woofly deciduous. The plain green kerria is a tall wiry plant covered in yellow balls in the spring. It is untidy and difficult to use successfully in a mixed scheme. The variegated version is quite different, as it develops into a small shrub that is more reluctant to flower than its larger

❀ *Hebe toparia* **makes a perfect companion plant for** *Abelia x grandiflora* **as well as a popular landing strip for a myriad of butterflies.**

Availability

☑ **Easily obtainable. Should be available anywhere.**

▣ **May require some searching or could be seasonal, but should not be too difficult to find.**

▦ **Best to order from a specialist nursery.**

Conditions **Sun or shade**
❋ **Shade**
❋ **Part shade**
❋ **Full sun**

relative. 90cm (3ft) with a similar spread.

▣ ❋ ❋ ❋ ▦ ▦ C G ◩ ◧

Lavenders

There are many different varieties of lavender on the market and you can become bogged down deciding which to choose. They tend to be planted at the front of a border, so size is the most important characteristic. The following three vary in size from the miniature 'Hidcote' to the large *L. angustifolia*. A white flowered variety might also be required in some schemes, in which case use *L. angustifolia* 'Alba' (large) or *L. angustifolia* 'Nana Alba' (small). All lavenders should be pruned immediately after flowering (usually in July and August) and again in the spring to maintain their shape. Always plant lavenders in the spring and look for fresh young plants.

Lavandula angustifolia (Lavender)

Woofly evergreen. This is the plain common or garden variety. It has pale lavender flowers and powdery grey foliage, and will quite often grow larger than expected. 1m (3ft 3in) with a similar spread.

☑ ❋ ▦ ▦ C G ◧

Lavandula angustifolia 'Hidcote' (Lavender)

Woofly evergreen. This is the one of the smallest lavenders and is often grown as a 'step-over' hedge around a flower bed. The flowers are a deeper colour than the species. Excellent around a rose bed. 60cm (2ft) with a similar spread.

☑ ❋ ▦ ▦ C M ◧

Lavandula angustifolia 'Munstead' (Lavender)

Woofly evergreen. This is the middle size of the three recommended. The flower colour is a deep purple. 80cm (2ft 6in) with a similar spread.

☑ ❋ ▦ ▦ C M ◧

Lonicera pileata

Horizontal evergreen. This small shrub, related to honeysuckle, is commonly used as a landscaping plant round municipal car parks. In the private garden it is useful because of its shape, which consists of a series of tiered horizontal branches. Use at the front of borders or as a structural plant at key points around the garden. 60cm (2ft) by 90cm (3ft).

☑ ❋ ❋ ❋ ❋ ▦ ▦ C G ◩ ◧

Magnolia × *soulangeana*

Woofly deciduous. Few deciduous trees and shrubs look as attractive as the magnolia in the winter, with its architectural framework of branches. The flowers, which appear in spring, are white, goblet-shaped and susceptible to late frost, which can completely destroy the display. Will eventually grow into a small tree. Try underplanting with cyclamen and grape hyacinth (*Muscari armeniacum*). 2m (6ft 6in) with similar spread.

☑ ❋ ❋ ▦ C P ◧

Magnolia stellata (Star magnolia)

Woofly deciduous. The smallest magnolia in regular use. The flowers, appearing in spring, are white and star-shaped, hence its common name, and have some resistance to frost. 1.5m (5ft) by 1.2m (4ft).

☑ ❋ ❋ ▦ C P ◧

Mahonia aquifolium 'Apollo' (Oregon grape)

Woofly evergreen. This tough little plant will grow almost anywhere, but can be a little bit scruffy and should only be used when nothing else will do. I always used to use *M. aquifolium* 'Atropurpurea' because of the purplish leaves in winter, but it has become so mixed in cultivation with the plain green variety that it is difficult to find. Although the effect in 'Apollo' is not quite as good, there is some useful winter colour in the leaves. The flowers are fragrant, yellow and grape-like, produced in March and April and followed by blue berries which persist into the autumn. To maintain a compact plant, it could be cut down to the ground each spring (a feed would be a good idea after this drastic action). 90cm (3ft) with a similar spread.

▣ ❋ ❋ ❋ ▦ ▦ C M ◩ ◧

Mahonia japonica, *M.* × 'Charity'

Horizontal/woofly evergreen. These mahonias are much larger and grander than the ordinary *M. aquifolium* varieties. The foliage is held in horizontal tiers and is accompanied by scented yellow flower spikes in mid-winter. They are not as tough as *M. aquifolium*. *M. Japonica* flowers earlier than 'Charity', perhaps even in early December, otherwise they are virtually the same plant. Where light reaches base of plant a 'skirt' will form, as long as pruning is avoided. 1.8m (6ft) by 1.5 m (5ft).

☑ ❋ ❋ ▦ C M ◩ ◧

Soil
PH Must have an acid soil
C Can cope with a light, dry sandy soil
C Grow well in clay soil
  Will grow in any soil, but not damp
  Will grow in damp or boggy conditions

Habit
G Good groundcover – the plant smothers the soil, stopping seeds from germinating.
M Some groundcover – the soil is covered but not enough to stop germination.
P Poor groundcover – there is a lot of bare soil around the plant.

Planting times (these represent the optimum time of the year to plant – for more details see page 12)
  Spring
  Autumn
  Summer

Osmanthus × burkwoodii (Sweet olive)
Round evergreen. Sweetly scented tiny white flowers in April mark this plant as one of the highlights of the spring. Position it where the scent can be enjoyed, perhaps beside a front door. Trim off the top growth to maintain its shape and encourage a 'skirt'. 1.2m (4ft) with a similar spread.

Osmanthus delavayi (Sweet olive)
Horizontal evergreen. This shrub has all the flowering attributes of its larger relatives, but on a smaller plant. The branches are tiered horizontally and there is no significant 'skirt'. 45cm (18in) by 60cm (2ft).

Pachysandra terminalis 'Variegata' (Japanese spurge)
Horizontal evergreen ground-cover. A useful plant for growing as a carpet in shade, it has proved to have many applications. Young plants can take their time to establish and are therefore best planted close together. Despite the fact that it is used in shade, it will grow in full sun and is used as a carpeting plant at Disneyland, Paris. Try growing it around the feet of fatsias. 10cm (4in) by 20cm (8in).

Paeonia suffruticosa (Tree peony)
Woofly deciduous. The large peony flowers of this plant can be any colour from white through pink, red to dark red, even yellow. The leaves have cut edges, giving the whole shrub a feathery appearance. 1.5m (5ft) by 1.2m (4ft).

Philadelphus (Mock orange blossom)
This genus provides the perfect example of why we should use the Latin name over the common name when ordering plants. The reason is that these plants vary considerably in size depending upon the variety – simply by asking for 'mock orange' could get you a petite plant growing to 90cm (3ft) high or a monster growing to 4m (13ft). Take a look at my selection:

Philadelphus 'Belle Etoile' (Mock orange blossom)
Ball-shaped deciduous. A reliable deciduous shrub making a stunning display of scented white flowers in May and June. 1.5m (5ft) with a similar spread.

Philadelphus 'Manteau d'Hermine' (Mock orange blossom)
A small deciduous shrub, perfect for small spaces and best grown in groups. White scented flowers are produced in May and June. 90cm (3ft) by 80 cm (2ft 6in).

Philadelphus × 'Virginal' (Mock orange blossom)
Perhaps the largest mock orange, growing to a height of 4 m (13ft) or even more in ideal conditions. The growth is very upright, with a small spread of around 1.2m (4 ft), making it an ideal plant where height is needed but space is limited. As with all mock oranges the flowers are white, scented and appear in May and June.

Phormium tenax (New Zealand flax)
Spiky evergreen. Often thought of as tender, I have found the plain green version of this plant very hardy indeed. In its native environment it grows in swamps and is just as happy in a dry soil as a very wet one. I have found it useful beside the River Great Ouse in a garden that is frequently under water. Not only does it cope with this fast-running river, but when the water level drops it is the only plant to emerge not covered in flotsam and jetsam. In the right conditions it will flower in mid-summer. The flowers are bronze-red and produced on spikes up to 4m (13ft). 1.5m (5ft) with a similar spread.

Phormium 'Bronze Baby' (New Zealand flax)
Spiky evergreen. This is a miniature phormium, more like a purple-leafed grass, but is not as tough as its plain green cousin and must have protection from winter winds. 60cm (2ft) by 80cm (2ft 6in).

Phormium 'Maori Sunrise' (New Zealand flax)
Spiky evergreen. This is a coloured version, which has red-purple, pink and bronze veining in the leaves. It is smaller than *P. tenax* and needs a sheltered position. 1m (3ft 3in) by 1.2m (4ft).

Photinia × fraseri 'Red Robin'
Woofly evergreen. This medium-sized shrub has bright red young growth in spring. 1.8m (6ft) by 1.5m (5ft).

Key to codes

Availability

☑ **Easily obtainable. Should be available anywhere.**

◨ **May require some searching or could be seasonal, but should not be too difficult to find.**

⌂ **Best to order from a specialist nursery.**

Conditions **Sun or shade**

❋ **Shade**

❋ **Part shade**

❋ **Full sun**

Pleioblastus auricoma. syn. *Arundinaria viridistriatus*
Upright evergreen. A small bamboo with yellowish green leaves. It is not invasive and makes a fine contrast to architectural plants like fatsia and *Mahonia japonica*. 1.2m (4ft) with a similar spread.

☑ ❋❋❋ ◨ ⬚ ▦ C P ◨ ◧

Potentillas

Related to roses, these plants have many uses in the garden. They have a long flowering period and come in colours ranging from white through yellow to orangy reds. The foliage is feathery, often with a powdery grey colour, and makes a fine contrast to many other leaf shapes. Each one of my selections has a different characteristic, thereby covering all the requirements from this genus, although I have avoided plants with red flowers as I find the colour does not combine well with other flowers.

Potentilla 'Abbotswood White' (Cinquefoil)
Ball-shaped deciduous. This is the largest of the potentillas recommended. It has largish white flowers for most of the summer. Good 'skirt'. 90cm (3ft) by 1.2m (4ft).

☑ ❋❋❋ ⬚ ▦ C G ◨ ◧

Potentilla fruticosa 'Manchu' (Cinquefoil)
Horizontal deciduous ground-cover. This is a wonderful plant, but can be difficult to obtain. It has grey foliage that hugs the ground, is covered by white flowers throughout the summer and it is perfect for growing close to a hot patio where it can sprawl across the flagstones. Care must be taken when buying this plant, as in most cases the plants are 'Abbotswood White' with the wrong label. 'Manchu' is easily recognized by its habit; it should be hugging the soil in the top of the pot, and even growing down the side. 15cm (6in) by 80cm (2ft 6in).

⌂ ❋❋ ⬚ ▦ C G ◨ ◧

Potentilla 'Tilford Cream' (Cinquefoil)
Ball-shaped deciduous. Produces creamy-yellow flowers for most of the summer. If top pruned it will develop a 'skirt'. 1m (3ft 3in) by 90cm (3ft).

◨ ❋❋❋ ⬚ ▦ C G ◨ ◧

Prunus lusitanica (Portuguese laurel)
Ball-shaped evergreen. Much more refined than cherry laurel (*P. laurocerasus*) but equally capable of growing in

most conditions. 1.8m (5ft) by 1.8m. Unpruned, it will form a 'skirt'.

☑ ❋❋❋ ⬚ ▦ C G ◨ ◧

Prunus lusitanica 'Variegata' (Portuguese laurel)
Ball-shaped evergreen. This is a white variegated version of the Portuguese laurel. Apart from the colour, its other virtue is that it is slower growing. May need some top pruning to encourage a 'skirt'. 1.5m (5ft) with a similar spread.

☑ ❋❋❋ ⬚ ▦ C G ◨ ◧

Rhamnus alaterna 'Argenteovariegata'
Ball-shaped evergreen. This relative of the native buckthorn is a large white-variegated shrub. It is thought to be slightly tender, but I have not found this a problem in Bedfordshire, although it does appear to grow better with its back against a south-facing wall. Unpruned, and happy, it will produce a very effective 'skirt'. 2.1m (7ft) by 2m (6ft 6in).

◨ ❋❋ ⬚ ▦ C G ◧

Roses

There are so many different varieties of roses in cultivation that they almost warrant a plant grouping on their own; it is sometimes difficult, faced with such diversity, to think of roses as just another shrub. They range in size from the tiny to enormous shrubs and ramblers; they come in every colour but one (no truly blue rose has yet been bred), and some of their flowers are not even the traditional rose shape.

Many people still believe that roses must be grown in monoculture beds, as the Victorians presented them, but this is a myth and denies the great versatility of this genus – in a mixed border they can extend the flowering season, in some cases from June through to the first frosts. Their presence can change the character of a garden, giving it a more English feel, and can even make it less formal. Despite what we are told, roses do not need pruning. In fact, all that is required is the removal of the 3 Ds – dead, diseased and dying wood. Any branches which fit these descriptions should be removed completely.

Classification of roses (floribunda, hybrid tea etc.) can be fairly haphazard, with the grower often deciding where a plant is pigeon-holed. This can lead to some plants with a variety of characteristics, finding themselves labelled differently in different catalogues. 'Little White Pet' is a good example: some catalogues list it as a shrub, others as a patio rose and sometimes a ground-cover shrub. Here I have shown the generally used classification. In

creative gardening for busy people

some instances I have recommended planting in the autumn; this is not because the roses cannot be planted in the spring, but the chances are that they will only be available bare-rooted for autumn planting.

Rosa 'Amber Queen'

Floribunda. Ball-shaped deciduous. Apart from the colour, this has to be the perfect rose. Its leaves are shiny and healthy and it flowers continually for six months without the need for deadheading. It even has a little scent. The flower colour, amber as the name suggests, is difficult to combine with other colours, although it does look good with lavender and *Salvia* 'East Friesland'. Can be a little fragile when young, so do not be surprised if there are losses. 60cm (2ft) by 45cm (18in).

Rosa 'Graham Thomas'

Shrub. Ball-shaped deciduous. This is one of the David Austin 'New English' roses and possibly the best. It is reliable in its flowering season, which is continuous, and fits in well with most styles of planting from the traditional rose bed through to the more informal mixed scheme. The flower colour is yellow and it makes a fine companion for spotted laurel, *Aucuba japonica* 'Variegata'. 1.2m (4ft) by 80cm (2ft 6in).

Rosa 'Little White Pet'

Shrub. Ball-shaped deciduous. This old rose, bred in 1879, is remarkable for its healthy disease-resistant foliage, so unusual on a rose from this era. The white pom-pom type flowers are preceded by red buds in flushes throughout the summer. Removal of deadheads helps this process. If left unpruned it will produce an acceptable 'skirt'. 60cm (2ft) with a similar spread.

Rosa 'Felicia'

Hybrid musk shrub. Ball-shaped deciduous. Hybrid musk roses are much under-used in the modern garden, which is a pity as they often flower for a long period and are generally trouble-free. Most are quite large, but this one only grows to a compact 1.2m (4ft) by 90cm (3ft). The flowers are pink and of the traditional rose shape. Grow with *Nepeta mussinii* and *Alchemilla mollis*.

Rosa 'Jacqueline du Pré'

Shrub. Ball-shaped deciduous. During field trials by one of the country's leading growers, a number of these were planted under an oak tree by mistake as part of a much larger exercise. After a length of time the other roses had deteriorated badly, some even dying, but the 'Jacqueline du Pré' was still doing well. As a result of this I have used this rose whenever the conditions are difficult and it has proved more than equal to the task. The flowers are white and appear over a long period. 1.2m (4ft) by 1m (3ft 3in) varying with the conditions.

Rosa 'Margaret Merril'

Floribunda. Ball-shaped deciduous. Floribundas in general are not known for their scent, but for their tendency to flower non-stop for long periods. This rose has the long-flowering characteristic, but unusually has won numerous awards for its scent. The flowers are flesh-pink. 80cm (2ft 6in) by 60cm (2ft).

Rosa rugosa alba.

Shub. Woofly deciduous. The rugosa roses are extremely useful for the country garden or in shady and difficult spots. If cut hard back in the spring they will remain reasonably compact, but they can be left to grow much larger. The flowers are large, white, clove-scented, and followed by large red hips in late

✿ *Rosa* **'Jacqueline du Pré'**

summer. By pruning annually the size can be maintained at 1.2m (4ft) with a similar spread. Left alone it will reach 1.8 m (6ft) with a similar spread and develop a very effective 'skirt'.

(unpruned)

Rosa rugosa 'Fru Dagmar Hastrup'

Shrub. Woofly deciduous. This red rugosa has similar attributes to *R. r. alba*, but may grow even larger if left unpruned. An

Key to codes

Availability
☑ Easily obtainable. Should be available anywhere.
🔎 May require some searching or could be seasonal, but should not be too difficult to find.
🔼 Best to order from a specialist nursery.

Conditions **Sun or shade**
✳ Shade
✳ Part shade
✳ Full sun

alternative is *Rosa rugosa* 'Scabrosa'.

🔎✳✳✳✳▦▣ⒸⒼ◨◲

Rosa 'Nevada'

Shrub. Ball-shaped deciduous. This plant is nothing like most people's idea of a rose: it is very large and the flowers are large, white and saucer-shaped. It flowers for most of the summer, although the first flush in June is the best. If left unpruned it will form a 'skirt'. 2m (6ft 6in) with a similar spread.

🔎✳✳✳✳▦▣ⒸⒼ◨◲

Rosmarinus officinalis, R. o. 'Miss Jessopp's Upright' (Rosemary).

Upright evergreen. A useful plant for the kitchen, and also a fine plant for the garden, where its upright grey foliage contrasts well with sage and *Alchemilla mollis*. 'Miss Jessopp's Upright' is more columnar. The flowers are blue and appear in early spring. 1.2m (4ft) with a similar spread (90cm (3ft).

☑✳✳✳▦▣ⒸⓂ◲

Ruta graveolens 'Jackman's Blue' (Rue)

Woofly evergreen. Most herbs do not make good garden plants, but this one is excellent. The foliage is powdery blue and combines well with roses, lavender and nepeta. Take care when handling it, as it can cause a rash with some people. 80cm (2ft 6in) by 70cm (2ft 3in).

☑✳✳✳▦▣ⒸⒼ◲

Salvia officinalis, S. o. 'Purpurascens', S. o. 'Icterina', S. o. 'Tricolor' (Sage)

Woofly, ball-shaped evergreen. The matt leaves of sage and its growing habit make it the perfect plant for both formal and informal arrangements. Planted close to a path or a paved area, it will tumble over the hard surface, softening and blurring the edge. Plant with rosemary and *Alchemilla mollis*. Can suffer in the winter, when the plant may open out and look untidy; if this happens cut it hard back and feed well. When ordering take care: ordinary sage is difficult to obtain as a large plant, but 'Purpurascens' is fairly similar and is always available as a larger specimen (the coloured sages are just as good as the plain sage in the kitchen). 'Icterina' has gold variegated foliage and 'Tricolor' white, pink and purple. 90cm (3ft) by 1.2m (4ft).

☑✳✳✳▦▣ⒸⒼ◲

Sambucus racemosa 'Plumosa Aurea' (Golden elder)

Woofly deciduous. As a plant, elder has a lot of desirable characteristics: feathery foliage, white flowers in the spring, followed by bunches of purple berries. Unfortunately it is a prolific weed, but there are some ornamental varieties available. The variety recommended here has more finely cut foliage than the native variety, and is a golden-yellow colour. It will grow in quite harsh shade, but the golden-yellow colour will almost certainly be lost; and full sun will scorch the foliage. Better to find a site in partial shade. Looks good alongside *Pleioblastus auricoma* or *Sarcococca humilis*. 2m (6ft 6in) with a similar spread.

☑✳✳ⒸⓂ◨◲

Sambucus racemosa 'Tenuifolia' (Green lace elder)

Woofly deciduous. From a distance this plant looks like a green Japanese maple (*Acer palmatum* 'Dissectum'). In fact it is much easier to grow than the maple, being able to cope with most conditions. A good companion for sage.
90cm (3ft) by 1.2m (4ft).

🔼✳✳✳✳▦▣Ⓒ✳Ⓖ◨◲

Sarcococca confusa (Christmas box)

Ball-shaped evergreen. The small white vanilla-scented flowers appear in January and are visually insignificant. Grow it near an often used doorway where the heady scent can best be enjoyed. 80cm (2ft 6in) with a similar spread. *S. humilis* is similar, but has a spreading habit.

☑✳✳✳▦ⒸⒼ◨◲

Spiraea nipponica 'Snowmound'

Weeping deciduous. This spring-flowering shrub has long arching stems of white flowers, giving the impression of a small fountain. 80cm (2ft 6in) with a similar spread.

☑✳✳✳▦▣ⒸⓂ◨◲

Stachyurus praecox

Ball-shaped deciduous. Occasionally something unusual and eye-catching is required and, if the conditions are right, this plant will provide just that with its unusual hanging cream-coloured flowers appearing on bare red-brown stems in late winter. It needs a rich woodland soil. 1.5m (5ft) with a similar spread.

🔼✳✳✳▦ⒸⒼ◨◲

Syringa meyeri 'Palabin', syn. S. velutina (Korean Lilac)

Woofly deciduous. In general, ordinary lilacs do not earn their keep, unless the garden is large enough to swallow them up, as they are large plants with greedy root systems and a short flowering season. This plant is the considered alternative. Its

Soil
- **PH** Must have an acid soil
- Can cope with a light, dry sandy soil
- **C** Grow well in clay soil
- Will grow in any soil, but not damp
- Will grow in damp or boggy conditions

Habit
- **G** Good groundcover – the plant smothers the soil, stopping seeds from germinating.
- **M** Some groundcover – the soil is covered but not enough to stop germination.
- **P** Poor groundcover – there is a lot of bare soil around the plant.

Planting times
(these represent the optimum time of the year to plant – for more details see page 12)
- Spring
- Autumn
- Summer

---

lilac-coloured flowers appear in May and June on a small twiggy plant, which looks best when planted in groups. 80cm (2ft 6in) with a similar spread.

☑ ❄ ✳ 🍂 C P 🍂 🍂

Teucreum fruticans (Shrubby germander)
Woofly evergreen. If you are looking for a plant that will flower non-stop from early spring through to autumn, look no further. It will need a sheltered sunny spot, however, or it may not survive the winter. The flowers are bright blue on long grey stems. A good companion for rosemary. 1m (3ft 3in) with a similar spread.

☑ ❄ 🍂 C M 🍂

Viburnum × carlesii
Ball-shaped deciduous. Of all the viburnums, and there are many varieties, this has the best scent. The flowers are white, opening from clusters of pink buds in April, and the foliage colours up brilliantly in the autumn. Slow-growing. 1.2m (4ft) with a similar spread.

○ ❄ ✳ 🍂 C M 🍂 🍂

Viburnum davidii
Horizontal evergreen. This viburnum has large leathery leaves and is often used in landscaping schemes. As a garden plant its shape and leaves contrast well with woofly deciduous plants. 90cm (3ft) by 1.4m (4ft 6in) (could be larger in ideal conditions).

☑ ❄ 🍂 ✳ 🍂 C G 🍂 🍂

Viburnum farreri
Upright deciduous. Winter colour is essential in any garden, and no plant provides more than this one. It begins flowering in the autumn and continues through to the spring, producing clusters of pink flowers during periods of warm weather. It also has the advantage of being taller than it is wide, making it perfect for hiding a fence in a small garden. 2.5m (8ft 3in) by 1.2m (4ft).

☑ ❄ ✳ 🍂 C P 🍂 🍂

Viburnum opulus 'Compactum' (Guelder rose)
Woofly deciduous. The ordinary guelder rose, a common hedgerow plant of the British countryside, is far too large and coarse for the small to average garden – it has a short flowering season and does not earn its keep. This plant, as the name suggests, is a miniature version. It forms a small ball-shaped shrub covered in attractive divided leaves which turn orange-red in the autumn. Clusters of white flowers cover the plant in late spring and early summer. V. o. 'Nanum' is similar, but it does not flower; a characteristic which helps it maintain a better shape.

80cm (2ft 6in) with a similar spread.

○ ❄ ✳ 🍂 🍂 C M 🍂 🍂

Viburnum plicatum 'Mariesii'
Horizontal deciduous. This large viburnum has horizontally tiered branches on which the lacecap-style flowers are also held in layers. It is a large spreading plant that is often not given enough space; a serious problem, as it should never be pruned. Grow in front of Laburnum anagyroides. 1.8m (6ft) by 2.4m (8ft).

○ ❄ ✳ 🍂 C G 🍂 🍂

Viburnum tinus, V. t. 'Variegata' (Laurustinus)
Ball-shaped evergreen. Possibly the longest continuous flowering season of any shrub, starting in October and going through to May. Despite this, the flowers are rather dull and tend to be ignored, the plant being grown for its solid evergreen foliage and easy-going nature. 2m (6ft 6in) with a similar spread ('Variegata' is slightly smaller). It will produce an effective 'skirt' if left unpruned.

☑ ❄ ✳ 🍂 🍂 C G 🍂 🍂

Vinca minor 'Atropurpurea' (Lesser periwinkle)
Horizontal evergreen ground-cover. The greater periwinkle, V. major, a robust colonizer, has given this plant an undeserved reputation. True, it will spread and overcome smaller plants, but most things are under little threat. It copes with quite harsh conditions and will form a useful, shiny, evergreen mat with delightful purple flowers in the spring. 15cm (6in) by 60cm (2ft).

☑ ❄ ✳ 🍂 🍂 C G 🍂 🍂

Yucca gloriosa (Adam's needle)
Spiky evergreen. White flowers on tall spikes are produced dramatically in August. Although it is usually planted in full sun, it can tolerate quite a lot of shade, coping well with any dryness in the soil. 1.5m (5ft) by 1.2m (4ft).

○ ❄ ✳ 🍂 🍂 C P 🍂 🍂

Bulbs

One of my first designs included an elaborate succession of flowering bulbs, starting in January with winter aconites and running through to May with tulips. These were followed by herbaceous perennials like geraniums and hostas, and the garden was magnificent for five months in the spring. The problem with bulbs, however, is that the leaves must be allowed to die down, and the dying foliage of the daffodils and tulips hung around well into June. My carefully designed planting scheme looked a mess.

135

Allowing the foliage to die down naturally is an important part of a bulb's cycle. It is at this time that the bulb is building its strength ready for flowering the next year (it is a good idea to remove any dying flower heads, as these take away much needed energy from the bulb). If the plant is not allowed to complete this cycle eventually it will stop flowering and become 'blind'. Daffodils and tulips are especially prone to this. There are many ways that gardeners deal with this dying off period: some tie the leaves into a knot, which is a curious way of dealing with the problem as it simply draws attention to it and certainly does no good. Another solution is to dig up the bulbs and heel them into an unused piece of ground with the intention of replanting them in the autumn. I did this once and forgot where I had heeled them in – ever since I have had a delightful clump of daffodils in the corner of the vegetable patch!

Back to the planting design. As the bulbs need time to die down naturally and moving them about can be a logistical problem, I now do not select bulbs which flower after March. These all tend to be smaller plants, so there is less foliage and the extra time allowed means they have completed their cycle before the summer perennials appear. If you already have later-flowering bulbs and feel that you cannot do without them, try planting them with a large, robust, deciduous perennial, the leaves of which will cover the bulb foliage as they die down. My favourite plant for this is *Hosta sieboldiana* 'Elegans', but *Geranium endressii* and *G.* 'Johnsons Blue' both do acceptable jobs.

The siting of bulbs in the garden is important. Many flower very early in the year, so it is pointless growing them where they are not going to be seen. Plant them close to a window, or in the front garden, where they can be best appreciated. If you are fortunate enough to have a patch in the garden which is bathed by the rising sun, then that is the place to plant daffodils. They will almost sing to you at breakfast.

In woodland areas, and under deciduous trees, bulbs come into their own. They complete their flowering cycle and die down before the tree canopy appears to deprive them of light. A carpet of winter aconites, snowdrops and species crocus is a delight in early spring. Bulbs can be naturalized in the lawn, but you must remember to allow the leaves to die down before cutting the grass in that area.

You may have noticed that I have not recommended tulips. This is mainly because they flower so late in the season that their dying leaves can be a problem, but also because their flowers look so unnatural in the mixed garden. Despite this, the dwarf species tulips make perfect specimens for colourful spring containers.

Planting

A common mistake when planting is to put the bulb in upside down. With some small bulbs it can be difficult to determine which is the top and which is the bottom, but generally the top is pointed and the bottom is flat with the remnants of the previous years' roots visible. If in doubt, ask at the garden centre or nursery where they were purchased.

The depth of planting is also important. Basically you plant the base of the bulb two and a half times deeper than the height of the bulb (this is only a rough measurement so there is no need to use a ruler).

Most can be bought and planted in a dry form, but snowdrops and winter aconites are more successful if planted in spring when there are still leaves on the plants. This is called 'in the green'.

Top 12 bulbs

Colchicum speciosum (Autumn crocus)
Autumn-flowering bulbs are often overlooked, possibly because this is the time of year to plant them, not to enjoy them. As the common name suggests, this plant is similar to the crocus. The leaves appear in spring and die down before the flowers are produced in the autumn.
Height 30cm (12in).
☑ ✦ ✦ ✦ ✦ Ⓒ ✦

Crocus tommasinianus (Crocus)
Modern varieties of crocus can look very artificial when they appear each spring, so I prefer to plant a species variety that looks more natural. This one has blue flowers from January to March and will spread readily. 10cm (4in).
◪ ✦ ✦ ✦ ✦ Ⓒ ▱

Cyclamen hederifolium
There are many different varieties of cyclamen, all very similar. This one is as good as any and is easy to obtain. It flowers on bare soil in the autumn and is followed by white-veined ivy-shaped leaves which persist throughout the winter. Try underplanting magnolias. 8cm (3in).
☑ ✦ ✦ ✦ Ⓒ ✦

Eranthis hyemalis (Winter Aconite)
This is the first bulb of the new season to flower, sometimes appearing in December. The flowers are yellow and appear above a ruff of feathery green foliage. Grow under trees as an accompaniment to snowdrops. Best planted in the spring when

the plants are still 'in the green'. 10cm (4in).

☑ ✳ ✳ ▨ C ◧

Erythronium dens-canis (Dog's tooth violet)

A wonderful little plant for a woodland area. Curiously, the bulbs move up or down in the soil until they have found their optimum level. In a flowerpot the bulbs will move through the hole in the bottom and into the soil underneath. Flowers are pink, purple or white and appear in spring. Plant early in autumn to ensure some root growth before winter. 30cm (12in).

⌂ ✳ ✳ ✳ ▨ C ▱

Galanthus nivalis (Snowdrop)

There are many different varieties of snowdrop, but most are distinguished only by subtle changes in the flower. Over a large area the effect is the same regardless of the variety. This is the native species and is easy to find. The flowers appear in January and combine well with eranthis and crocus. 15cm (6in).

☑ ✳ ✳ ✳ ▨ ▨ C ◧

Lilium martagon (Turk's cap lily)

This delightful lily will naturalize itself if the conditions are right. Its distinctive Turk's head shape is perfect in a woodland setting. It may not flower in its first season. Up to 1.5m (5ft).

⌂ ✳ ✳ ✳ ▨ C ▱

Muscari armeniacum (Grape hyacinth)

This bulb can be very invasive, so it needs careful placing in the garden. Its leaves appear in the autumn and persist throughout the winter, to be followed by blue flowers in early spring. Looks good around the feet of spring-flowering magnolias. 20cm (8in).

☑ ✳ ✳ ✳ ▨ ▨ C ▱

Narcissus 'February Gold'

Daffodil. This medium-sized daffodil flowers early in the season; although normally this is in March not February, unless the season is particularly early. It dies down comparatively quickly after flowering and is easy to obtain. *Narcissus* 'February Silver' is a white-flowered version. 45cm (18in).

☑ (▱ for 'Silver') ✳ ✳ ✳ ▨ C ▱

Narcissus 'Thalia'

A small, refined white daffodil for jobs which need smaller plants than *N.* 'February Silver'. 30cm (12in).

▱ ✳ ✳ ✳ ▨ C ▱

Nerine bowdenii

Few plants flower solely in November. The bright pink flowers make a very summer-like display at a time when only autumn colours prevail. It needs full sun, preferably beside a wall where it can bake. It can become a little invasive, so care should be taken to ensure that its neighbours are robust. 45cm (18in).

☑ ✳ ▨ ▨ C ✳

Scilla sibirica (Siberian squill)

This plant is like a miniature bluebell. It looks good naturalized or growing in scree beds. 8cm (3in).

☑ ✳ ✳ ✳ ▨ ▨ C ▱

Trees

Trees are the largest living things in any garden and can also, potentially, be the largest problem; it is critical therefore to select the right tree from the outset. Too many people plant trees that are too large for the space available, believing that they can simply remove them if they get too large. It is amazing how quickly a tree can grow – before anyone has noticed, it needs dealing with and it is then that the owner discovers the high costs involved in removing a mature specimen.

Choosing a tree

Large trees like oak, willow, ash, lime, beech, chestnut, etc. should not be planted close to a building; the exact distance is one of judgement and will depend on the foundations of the building as much as anything else. Most new houses will have deep and substantial foundations. Despite that I would err on the side of caution and only plant a large tree in a significantly large garden and then as far from the house as possible. The problems of a large tree in a small garden are infinite.

Buying a tree

During the dormant period, between October and March, deciduous trees and shrubs can simply be dug from the ground, the soil removed from their roots and the plants transported to a new position. Until the advent of the plastic flower pot, all deciduous trees and shrubs had to be bought from nurseries in this way; they would be ordered throughout the summer and dispatched during the winter months. Now, apart from some of the more unusual roses, everything can be purchased already growing in pots. However, trees are still available bare-rooted and are generally much better specimens than those grown in containers. This also enables you to buy larger, more mature plants at a better price.

Key to codes

Availability
☑ **Easily obtainable. Should be available anywhere.**
▣ **May require some searching or could be seasonal, but should not be too difficult to find.**
⬆ **Best to order from a specialist nursery.**

Conditions **Sun or shade**
✳ **Shade**
✲ **Part shade**
❋ **Full sun**

How to order and what to order

It should be possible to order bare-rooted plants through your local garden centre, but it would be better to find a nursery which specializes in bare-rooted stock (there are some useful addresses at the back of this book, or in *The Plant Finder*). Decide what size you want. It is possible to buy bare-rooted trees up to 4.5m (14ft 9in) in height (larger plants will be available, but the cost will jump, as moving anything that large involves a lot more work), but you must bear in mind that the larger the plant the fewer varieties will be available so you must be prepared to be more conservative in your selection. Check with the nurseryman to find out what he has and the sizes available.

Also, it's useful to to know that larger trees tend to be more slow-growing than smaller ones – in fact, the smaller the plant the faster it will grow, suggesting that at a point in the future two trees of the same variety, one large, one small, will eventually be the same size.

So why go to the expense of planting a large tree, when a cheaper, smaller one will grow to the same height? Two reasons. First, the larger plant will give you an instant tree, which could be useful for screening or for adding instant maturity, and secondly, being more slow-growing could be useful if space is limited.

Planting a tree

A tree must be supported in its early years of life, and this is best done with a stake. If you do not secure a tree, the wind will cause the roots to rock loose, air will get between the roots and the soil, and the plant will starve to death.

The modern method of staking is to use a small stake – this allows the plant to move with the wind and is said to help it create a stronger root system. This is fine for a bare-rooted tree, but I have found that plants grown in small pots can develop weak stems and snap off just above the stake. I always recommend that a pot-grown plant be supported using a full-sized stake. Also, windy sites can be a problem. If there is a constant prevailing wind, the tree can grow with a bad 'lean' using the small stake method.

Large specimen trees will probably require a more solid form of support than a single stake. Ask the supplier what he or she recommends.

When staking, ensure where possible that the support is on the windward side of the plant (usually south-west). This ensures that the tree braces away from the support and does not rub against it. It is essential that the tie used to secure the tree to the stake be loosened as the plant grows, or it will cut into the bark and may do substantial damage to the young tree.

Existing trees

These can often be important to a new garden, as they offer maturity which would otherwise take many years to achieve. Having said this, a poorly placed tree can totally upset a garden, and spending time trying to incorporate something which is so plainly wrong is a waste of time. Either get rid of

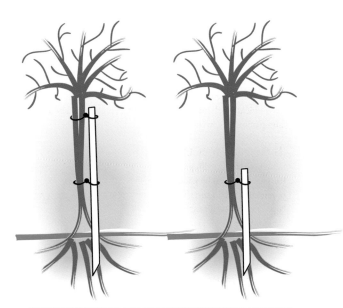

| Full stake | Short stake |

it or move it. Move it? Yes, move it. Capability Brown, the great eighteenth century landscape gardener, would not have thought twice about moving a mature oak tree on the back of a horse-drawn cart if it was in the wrong place. Any deciduous plant can be moved during its dormant period simply by lifting it out of the ground, brushing the soil from the roots and taking it to its new position. The trick is having the facilities, either in manpower or in machinery, to carry out the move. Many companies now have what are called 'tree-spades' – large twin blades, usually attached to the back of a lorry, which scoop the plant out of the ground and lay it on the lorry for transportation.

I make it sound easy, and it is, so long as the space is available for the machinery to gain access. It won't be cheap, but will certainly cost less than purchasing a similar tree of the same size. Frankly, moving large trees is done only as a last resort.

Maintenance

Occasionally it is necessary to reduce a tree's size, either to keep it in bounds or because it has become dangerous. It is important that this work is carried out by a qualified tree surgeon, otherwise the tree may be so badly damaged that it loses its shape or even its life. I see too many trees that have been reduced by simply chopping the top off – it makes them unsightly and in most cases they will not recover their original shape.

If you have old, larger specimens you should ask a tree surgeon to have a close look at them periodically. There may be problems which are not visible from the outside and which will need an expert's eye to spot; in most cases problems can be fixed fairly quickly with little expense. The alternative could be a falling branch or, even worse, a whole tree.

Trees as weeds

Sometimes tree seedlings appear in the garden, usually grown from seeds carried by wind or animals; these represent a potential problem and should be removed before they get too large. The main culprits are ash, sycamore, oak and horse chestnut, but almost any tree can be a nuisance in this way.

Top 20 trees

The following is a list of trees that offer a lot to the ornamental garden, are not difficult to obtain and are easy to grow. They are not all small trees and some will require considerable space. The size that a tree will reach is very difficult to ascertain, much more so than with other plants. The sizes shown are, as with everything in this book, an anticipated size after approximately eight years, but this could vary considerably.

Acer pseudoplatanus 'Leopoldii'

Lollipop-shaped deciduous. The variegated Norway maple, *A. platanoides* 'Drummondii', has become very popular in recent years and has been planted in many small gardens. The problem is that some of its branches will revert to plain green, and if they are not removed, eventually this happens to the whole plant. *A. pseudoplatanus* 'Leopoldii' is a larger plant, but it has reliable creamy-white-variegated foliage which rarely reverts; altogether

a much better tree. Although related to sycamore, it does not get as large; but it can reach two-thirds the height of a sycamore given fifty or sixty years. 4m (13ft) with a similar spread.

🔾 ✳ ✳ ☒ ☒ C

Acer campestre (Field maple)

Lollipop-shaped deciduous. This common hedgerow tree should not be overlooked simply because of where it grows in the countryside, as it is a fine plant for a small garden. The foliage is attractive, being an interesting palm-like shape, and the autumn colour is good. The perfect choice for the traditional country garden. 3m (9ft 10in) with a similar spread.

🔾 ✳ ✳ ✳ ☒ ☒ C

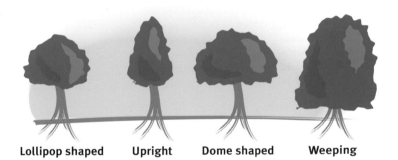

Lollipop shaped   **Upright**   **Dome shaped**   **Weeping**

Tree shapes

Aesculus × carnea (Red horse chestnut)

Lollipop-shaped deciduous. Few trees can boast the floriferous display of the horse chestnut in spring. This is a large tree, but not as large as the white-flowered variety. The blooms are sweetly scented, if you can get close enough to them. 5m (16ft) with a similar spread.

🔾 ✳ ✳ ☒ ☒ C

Betula jacquemontii (Silver birch)

Upright deciduous. For white bark this is the best birch. Silver birch are fast-growing and have a very light canopy so that underplanting is not deprived of light. 4m (13ft) by 3m (9ft

Key to codes

Availability
☑ **Easily obtainable. Should be** available anywhere.
◨ **May require some searching or** could be seasonal, but should not be too difficult to find.
⌂ **Best to order from a specialist** nursery.

Conditions **Sun or shade**
✳ **Shade**
✳ **Part shade**
✳ **Full sun**

10in). *B.j.* 'Grayswood Ghost' has particularly fine white bark.

☑ ✳ ✳ ✳ 🖐 ▦ C

Betula nigra (River birch)

Upright deciduous. Occasionally I come across a garden which has a high water table, or even a rising and falling water table,

❀ **Reverted Norway maple.**

and this calls for a tree which can cope with these conditions. The choice is fairly limited, including willow, alders and swamp cypress, but river birch is a good choice for a small garden. 4m (13ft) by 3m (9ft 10in).

⌂ ✳ ✳ ✳ ◐ 🖐 ▦ C

Catalpa bignonioides (Indian bean tree)

Dome-shaped deciduous. This almost exotic-looking tree benefits from large heart-shaped leaves and a wide spreading dome shape as it matures. Although not particularly tall, it can spread a fair distance sideways. If coppiced annually it can be kept as a medium-sized shrub and the leaves will double in size. The white-flecked flowers appear in mid-summer, followed by long black pods in the autumn. 4m (13ft) with a similar spread.

◨ ✳ ✳ 🖐 C

Cotoneaster 'Cornubia'

Lollipop-shaped evergreen. The large-leafed cotoneasters are very useful plants in the garden despite being a little boring. They can be trained as shrubs and even make a good hedge, but as small trees they have no equals. This is simply because there are few evergreen broad-leafed trees available to garden-makers in the British Isles. Holly can be grown as a small tree, but it is very slow-growing. The flowers in mid-summer are insignificant, but the red berries that appear in late summer last

into the winter. 3m (9ft 10in) with a similar spread.

◨ ✳ ✳ ✳ 🖐 ▦ C

Crataegus oxyacantha 'Paul's Scarlet', *C. o.* 'Rosea Flore Pleno' (Hawthorn)

Lollipop-shaped deciduous. Hawthorn makes a fine tree for most gardens and in most settings, but is especially good in a country garden, where it helps considerably in providing a link with the surrounding country. It is tough, coping with almost any conditions. The flowers appear in May – red on 'Paul's Scarlet', pink on 'Rosea Flore Pleno' – and the leaves colour up well in the autumn. The canopy on mature trees is rather dense, making it good for screening but difficult to plant underneath. 3m (9ft 10in) with a similar spread. If buying a mature specimen, do not buy anything large than 3m as beyond this size hawthorn does not transplant well.

☑ ✳ ✳ ✳ 🖐 ▦ C

Juglans regia (Walnut)

Lollipop-shaped deciduous. Anyone with enough space should plant a walnut, not for the nuts, which are produced only on mature trees of 15–20 years of age, but for its overall shape and silver grey bark. Eventually it will grow as large as any forest tree, but allow 4m (13ft) initially, with a similar spread.

☑ ✳ ✳ 🖐 C

Laburnum anagyroides (Golden rain, Common laburnum)

Upright deciduous. This tree has suffered a bad press in recent years because of its poisonous seed pods, but there are many plants more poisonous which we grow in the garden without concern. The golden hanging flowers appear in May on a tree which is tolerant of most conditions. 3m (9ft 10in) by 2.5m (8ft 2in).

⌂ ✳ ✳ ✳ 🖐 ▦ C

Laburnum x *watereri* 'Vossii' (Golden Rain, Voss's laburnum)

Identical in almost every way to *L. anagyroides*, but has fewer pods, flowers in June rather than May and is easier to obtain. As I like to grow laburnums with *Viburnum plicatum* 'Mariesii', the late flowering spoils the effect. 3m (9ft 10in) by 2.5m (8ft 2in).

☑ ✳ ✳ ✳ 🖐 ▦ C

plant lists

Soil
- **PH** Must have an acid soil
- Can cope with a light, dry sandy soil
- **C** Grow well in clay soil
- Will grow in any soil, but not damp
- Will grow in damp or boggy conditions

Habit
- **G** Good groundcover –the plant smothers the soil, stopping seeds from germinating.
- **M** Some groundcover – the soil is covered but not enough to stop germination.
- **P** Poor groundcover – there is a lot of bare soil around the plant.

Planting times
(these represent the optimum time of the year to plant – for more details see page 12)
- Spring
- Autumn
- Summer

Liquidambar styraciflua (Sweet gum, Satinwood)

Upright deciduous. Eventually this will make a very large parkland plant, 30m (100 ft) plus in height. The autumn colours can be staggering, especially in lime-free soil, making this plant a 'must' for a garden large enough. 4m (13ft) by 3m (9ft 10in).

Liriodendron tulipiferum (Tulip tree)

Upright deciduous. An interesting medium to large tree which produces large tulip-shaped white flowers on mature specimens (it can take twenty years before the first flowers appear). The foliage consists of unusual three-pointed leaves. 4m (13ft) by 3m (9ft 10in).

Mespilus germanica (Medlar)

Dome-shaped deciduous. This small garden tree has a wonderful architectural shape, forming a low, squat mushroom. The fruits are an acquired taste and must be rotten before they can be eaten. 2.5m (8ft 2in) with a similar spread.

Morus nigra (Mulberry)

Lollipop-shaped deciduous. This small tree, although associated with period gardens, should be considered for any small garden. The leaves colour up well in the autumn and are accompanied by the almost black raspberry-like fruits (which can be a problem as they make a nasty mess below the tree when ripe). Although it will grow in open ground it is happiest in front of a south facing wall or fence. 2.5 m (8ft 2in) with a similar spread.

Prunus subhirtella 'Autumnalis' (Winter-flowering cherry)

Lollipop-shaped deciduous. Flowers in winter are always appreciated and this plant produces pink ones from October to March on bare stems. Coupled with the summer leaves, the effect is a tree that has all-year-round interest. The flowering is not continuous, with breaks caused by severe weather, and young plants generally have a poor shape. Avoid top-grafted trees, a method designed to produce a more mature plant without having to wait for it to grow – the result is unnatural and unsatisfactory. 4m (13ft) with a similar spread.

Prunus serrula (Paperbark cherry)

Lollipop-shaped deciduous. When talking about trees the effect created by the trunk is rarely considered, but some tree trunks can be a delight. For instance, London plane trees, walnuts and elms all have trunks that demand closer scrutiny. Silver birch and the paper-bark maples (*Acer griseum*) are both small garden trees renowned for the colour of their bark. The paper-bark maple has flaking chocolate-coloured bark, making it one of the most attractive trees for the small garden – the problem is that it is so slow-growing that it is virtually impossible to obtain a plant of any size and what is available is costly. The alternative is the paperbark cherry, which has mahogany-coloured peeling bark. 4m (13ft) with a similar spread.

Pyrus salicifolia 'Pendula' (Weeping pear)

Weeping deciduous. Weeping trees have always attracted the unwary gardener, who usually looks towards the willows – either the monster weeping willow (*Salix babylonica*) or the diminutive Kilmarnock willow (*S. caprea* 'Pendula'). The curious thing about the weeping willow is that most people know it is too large for their garden but feel they can control it. In reality the growth is always faster than expected, leaving the garden owner with huge bills for having it removed or repairing any damage the roots might cause. The Kilmarnock willow has the opposite problem in that it is too small, making it difficult to place in a design. The weeping pear, however, is an excellent alternative, with attractive grey foliage on a comparatively small plant. Grow with red rugosa roses for a stunning effect. 3m (9ft 10in) with a similar spread.

Robinia pseudoacacia 'Frisia' (False acacia, golden locust)

Upright deciduous. A very useful, if overplanted, ornamental tree. Its yellow foliage is soft and subtle, making the perfect contrast for purples and blues. Try planting on the western side of the garden to enjoy the setting sun lighting up the foliage from behind. Plant a group of *Elaeagnus pungens* 'Maculata' at its feet for a memorable effect. It suffers from being very brittle, so should be avoided in exposed gardens. 3m (9ft 10in) by 2.5m (8ft 2in). *Gleditzia triacanthos* 'Sunburst', the honey locust, is a very similar plant, but also suffers from the same brittleness.

Sorbus aucuparia (Rowan, Mountain Ash)

Lollipop-shaped deciduous. This fine tree has everything: flowers

Key to codes

Availability
☑ Easily obtainable. Should be available anywhere.
◻ May require some searching or could be seasonal, but should not be too difficult to find.
🏠 Best to order from a specialist nursery.

Conditions **Sun or shade**
❋ Shade
❋ Part shade
❋ Full sun

in early summer, attractive foliage that colours well in autumn and clusters of attractive orange berries. This is the common rowan, although there are many types, some with pink, others with white berries. It will grow almost anywhere, but is best in an open position. 3m (9ft 10in) with a similar spread. One warning: Sorbus splits into two groups: the rowans and the whitebeams. Whitebeam, *S. aria*, is a fine tree in its own right, but it has a very dense canopy, making it very difficult to plant under, or near.

☑ ❋ ❋ ❋ ❋ ❋ C

✿ **The bright yellow leaves of** Robinia pseudoacacia **'Frisia' will light up in the evening sun.**

Conifers

There have been far too many conifers planted in this country over the last thirty years – so many that they have earned a poor reputation. In many instances their shape and style are in conflict with both the local flora and architecture, but this has not stopped them from being planted without any thought.

Most conifers will not recover from damage to their foliage, so are not suitable for planting in a mixed scheme as neighbouring plants lean against them and cut out the light. This lack of recovery is caused by most conifers lacking any dormant buds in their old wood, so once the foliage has died it cannot be replaced. If you want to remove an unwanted plant, there will be no regrowth once the foliage has been removed.

The exception to this is yew (*Taxus baccata*), which can, in theory, be cut back to the main trunk from where dormant buds will shoot. I say 'in theory' because it is not a good idea to remove all the green foliage from any evergreen in one go. If it is the intention to cut a yew back to the main trunk, then this should be done in stages.

In the garden, conifers are useful for ground-cover

and for adding the upright, or fastigiate, shape. But take care, ground-cover plants can be very vigorous and could grow much larger and faster than expected. Also, few conifers improve with age; they tend to become untidy and open, and even, as in the case of pines, lose their lower branches as they develop.

The size of some conifers puts them into the same bracket as the large deciduous forest trees mentioned on pages 137-142, and should not be planted close to a building or in a small garden. The most commonly planted 'mistakes' are larch, Scots and Austrian pine.

Top 20 conifers

Chamaecyparis pisifera 'Filifera Aurea'

Weeping evergreen. This gold-leafed conifer is excellent for banks, or beside water where its foliage can trail over the edge. It is slow-growing, but allow for 80cm (2ft 6in) by 90cm (3ft). *C. p.* 'Sungold' is similar.

◻ ❋ ❋ ❋ C G ❋ ❋

Ginkgo biloba (Maidenhair tree)

Upright deciduous. It is difficult to believe that this ancient plant is a conifer, as it has deciduous broad leaves and an open-branched habit. The foliage turns a butter yellow in the autumn. Treat it as if it were a broad-leafed tree and expect to be able to plant up to its trunk, as there will be no 'skirt'. 6m (20ft) by 3m (10ft).

◻ ❋ ❋ ❋ C P ❋ ❋

Juniperus chinensis 'Pyramidalis'

Upright evergreen. This slow-growing conifer forms a solid column of blue green foliage. It would not be happy with too much foliage close by which could cause die-back, but looks good with low-growing plants. 1.2m (4ft) by 60cm (2ft). *J. c.* 'Stricta' is identical.

◻ ❋ ❋ C M ❋ ❋

Juniperus communis 'Compressa'

Upright evergreen. It can be difficult to incorporate all the plant shapes into miniature landscapes, and this plant is one of the few rock plants which has an upright or fastigiate shape. It would not be happy leaning against anything, but looks good with ground-covering alpines. 60cm (2ft) by 10cm (4in).

◻ ❋ ❋ ❋ C P ❋ ❋

Juniperus communis 'Green carpet'

Horizontal evergreen. Groundcovering conifers all seem to suffer from the same problem – they have too large a spread. This one is better-behaved. 15cm (6in) by 1m (3ft 3in).

Juniperus sabina 'Tamariscifolia' (Shore juniper)

Horizontal evergreen. This ground-covering conifer requires space, but is a good choice for growing on a bank. As it grows across the ground it throws up small peaks which are very effective on a sloping surface.
15cm (6in) by 1.5m (5 ft).

Juniperus squamata 'Blue Star'
(Scaly-leafed Nepal juniper)

Horizontal evergreen. Another well-behaved ground-cover conifer; it is so slow-growing that planting in a group of three is sometimes the only way to achieve the size required. The foliage is blue green in colour. 30cm (1ft) by 60cm (2ft).
J. s. 'Holger' is a plain green version.

Juniperus scopulorum 'Skyrocket' (Pencil juniper)

Upright evergreen. As the common name suggests, this plant is very narrow in its growth habit. 1.5m (5ft) by 50cm (15in).

Picea pungens 'Maculata' (Blue spruce)

Horizontal evergreen. Although listed as horizontal, this refers to its growth habit rather than to any ground-covering qualities. The blue spruces are very popular with gardeners, but they often buy a plant that is far too large for their garden. This one is a dwarf variety and perfect for the small garden. 90cm (3ft) by 60cm (2ft).

Taxodium distichum (Swamp cypress)

Upright deciduous. One of the few deciduous conifers, this plant, as the name suggests, likes to grow with its feet in wet soil – although this is not essential. It is the perfect choice for growing beside a lake or river where its roots will spread out under the water. 5m (16ft) by 2.5m (8ft).

Taxus baccata (Yew)

Woofly evergreen. Yew is the king of hedging plants and should be the first choice for any garden. It can be trimmed to almost any shape and its matt green foliage is the perfect foil for other plants. Yew is renowned for being slow-growing, but if the ground is heavily fertilized and the root system receives plenty of water it will grow quite quickly. If the leading growth is removed it will form a 'skirt'. Yew is poisonous and should not be planted where horses are likely to graze. 1.2m (4ft) with a similar spread.

Taxus baccata 'Fastigiata' (Irish yew)

Upright evergreen. Unlike other upright conifers, this one can cope happily with close planting. It has a tendency to fatten out at the base as it grows, but this can easily be trimmed to maintain the desired shape. 1.2m (4ft) by 50cm (15in). *Taxus baccata* 'Fastigiata Aurea' is similar but with golden foliage.

Taxus baccata 'Repandens' (Prostrate yew)

Horizontal evergreen. This low-growing yew is one of the few groundcover conifers for shade. 1.2m with a similar spread.

Taxus baccata 'Repens Aurea'
(Prostrate golden yew)

Horizontal evergreen. Like 'Repandens', but with golden foliage and appears to grow even lower. Looks good in scree beds.

Taxus baccata 'Summergold' (Yew)

Woofly evergreen. This golden yew, if left unpruned, develops a 'goblet' shape. It is reasonably well-behaved and useful for marking key points in the garden. 1.2m (4ft) with a similar spread.

Thuja occidentalis 'Rheingold'

Woofly evergreen. This popular conifer comes into its own in the spring, when its golden foliage appears to shine in the early summer sunshine. Grow *Berberis thunbergii* 'Atropurpurea Nana' around its feet for a stunning effect. 1.5m (5ft) by 90cm (3ft).

Thuja occidentalis 'Smaragd' (White cedar)

Upright evergreen. A narrow upright column, with interesting

Key to codes

Availability
☑ **Easily obtainable. Should be available anywhere.**
▣ **May require some searching or could be seasonal, but should not be too difficult to find.**
▣ **Best to order from a specialist nursery.**

Conditions **Sun or shade**
▨ **Shade**
▨ **Part shade**
▨ **Full sun**

'spiralling' in the foliage. 1.2m (4ft) by 50cm (15in).

▣ ▨ ▨ ▨ C P ▨ ▨

Thuja orientalis 'Aurea Nana'

Ball-shaped evergreen. This plant forms a complete ball shape, almost like a large lollipop, with golden foliage. Must be grown as a specimen, as it is not happy with foliage close by. Will grow slowly to 80cm (2ft 6in) by 60cm (2ft). No 'skirting'.

☑ ▨ ▨ C ▨ ▨

Thuja plicata (Western red cedar)

Before the advent of the leylandii conifer, this is the plant which was planted as a fast-growing hedge. Nowhere near as fast as leylandii, it does grow quite quickly and makes a much better hedge. As a free-standing plant, it has a pleasing shape for such a large tree; almost like a teardrop. 2.5m (8ft) by 80cm (2ft 6in). In time will reach 50 metres.

☑ ▨ ▨ ▨ ▨ C G ▨ ▨

Thujopsis dolobrata (Hiba)

Woofly evergreen. This fabulously architectural plant is an unusual addition to any garden. It has no objection to other plants growing against it, and is extremely tough, growing in almost any conditions. In the wild it will grow to 30 metres in height, but in cultivation will develop into a sprawling shrub, which will respond to pruning, should it be necessary. 1.5m (5ft) by 1.2m (4ft).

▣ ▨ ▨ ▨ ▨ C M ▨ ▨

Climbers and wall shrubs

The importance of vertical planting in the garden is often over-looked. It is a good, quick way of introducing height, maturity and screening. Many garden structures, for example pergolas and summerhouses, benefit from softening by climbers.

Most climbers must be robust enough to cover a structure: a fence, a pergola etc. and may need some pruning to keep them within bounds – a necessary evil to achieve the desired coverage. Less robust climbers, perhaps grown more for their flowers, are better grown through other climbers or shrubs. This will give them the necessary support, both physically and visually.

Only a handful of climbers are self-clinging – the rest will need something to cling, or be tied, to. Many people use trellis attached to the wall, but this can be a problem as the support then becomes a feature on its own and interferes with the display of the plant it is meant to support. Much better to use galvanized wire and vine eyes; as the metal oxidizes it blends into the background and does not interfere with the display of the plants.

Top 50 climbers and wall shrubs

Abutilon megapotamicum (Flowering maple)

Deciduous lax shrub. There are a number of readily available varieties like 'Kentish Belle' and 'Ashford Red', all of which flower from summer into autumn; the flowers are hanging, bell-shaped and usually of two different colours. The plant is very lax needing some support to be effective, and must be backed by a hot sunny wall. 2.4m (8ft) with a similar spread (it is easy to keep in bounds and will probably be held back by cold winter weather anyway).

▣ ▨ ▨ ▨ C ▨ ▨

✿ **The trellis here is dominating the scene, drawing attention away from the rose.**

Actinidia kolomikta

Deciduous rambler. This large climber has unusual pink-variegated foliage. It really needs a warm situation, ideally in full sun, although I have seen it growing reasonably well against a north-facing fence. It can be slow growing to start with, but once established, and happy with its situation, it can be quite robust. 3m (9ft 10in) with a similar spread.

▣ ▨ ▨ ▨ ▨

Akebia quinata (Chocolate vine)

Deciduous rambler. This plant is extremely useful because it is fast-growing from a standing start, whereas most climbers take some time to get their roots set before beginning their journey. It has a fairly light foliage system, making it perfect for the front uprights of a pergola, or among other climbers. Grow it alongside a grape vine on a new pergola – the akebia will sprint to the top and provide instant colour and the vine

✿ **Vine eyes and galvanized wire are tidy and unseen.**

will follow along later and take over. The flowers are chocolate-purple in colour, appearing in April, and, despite being deciduous, it retains its leaves well into the winter and is one of the first plants to break into leaf the following spring. 5m (16ft) with a similar spread.

Azara dentata

Evergreen shrub. The sweetly scented yellow flowers of this shrub are a delight in early spring, but it must have a warm, sheltered situation, as it is not reliably hardy. 2.4m (8ft) by 1.5m (5ft).

Ceanothus 'Concha' (Californian lilac)

Evergreen shrub. Everyone loves the bright blue flowers of ceanothus, which are a highlight of the spring; this is one of the best, although any of the shrubby wall varieties will do. Avoid *C. thrysiflorus* 'Repens', which is a wide-spreading ground-cover plant and the deciduous varieties like 'Gloire de Versailles' which are free-standing plants. 3m (9ft 10in) with a similar spread.

Ceanothus 'A.T. Johnson' (Californian Lilac)

Evergreen shrub. A similar plant to 'Concha', but also flowers again in the autumn.

Clematis

To flower well, clematis need to ripen their flowering wood, and to do this they need it to be in full sun; they also need their feet in cool shade and plenty of water in dry weather. Many will grow on a north-facing wall, but their wood will not ripen and flowering is poor or non-existent. I have found the large-flowered hybrids the most difficult to grow and they are best avoided; the clematis suggested below are reasonably accommodating and make a reliable display every year. All can suffer from a disease called clematis wilt, which can strike at any time and will kill young plants. Always destroy any dead foliage completely, or remove it from the garden, and plant the plants with the top of the pot-soil 10cm (4in) below the soil; if wilt strikes, the plant will re-grow from below the ground.

Clematis alpina, C. macropetala

Deciduous rambler. With careful selection it is possible to have clematis flowering for ten months of the year and these are the ones which flower in April and May. The flowers are bell-shaped and predominantly blue, although colours range from white through to pink, depending upon the variety. These are also among the smallest-growing climbers and make good specimens for containers. 3m (9ft 10in) with a similar spread.

Clematis armandii

Evergreen rambler. This is one of the few true climbing evergreens which is reliably hardy in the British Isles. In northern counties it will require a south-facing, protected wall, but further south, it will grow almost anywhere, once established. In fact, in ideal conditions, it can be a rampant nuisance. The flowers appear in April. 5m (16ft) with a similar spread.

Clematis cirrhosa balearica

Evergreen rambler. This is the other evergreen clematis. It flowers throughout the winter months whenever the weather is mild, with small white cup-shaped flowers, and the foliage is small with a fern-like appearance. It needs some protection, either from a warm wall or by growing through border shrubs. It is useful for disguising a waterbutt – surround the butt with chicken wire for support. 2.4m (8ft) with a similar spread.

Clematis flammula (Fragrant virgin's bower)

Deciduous rambler. This vigorous climber has heavily scented, white flowers, which appear in late summer and autumn. Ideal for an arbour over a garden seat. 3m (10ft) with a similar spread.

Availability

☑ **Easily obtainable. Should be available anywhere.**

▢ **May require some searching or could be seasonal, but should not be too difficult to find.**

▢ **Best to order from a specialist nursery.**

Conditions **Sun or shade**

❋ **Shade**

❋ **Part shade**

❋ **Full sun**

Clematis 'Jackmanii Superba'

Deciduous rambler. This is a largish-flowered clematis and one I have found to be reliable and easy to grow; the flowers are dark purple and appear from mid-summer to autumn. 3m (10ft) with a similar spread.

Clematis 'Marie Boisselot'

Deciduous rambler. A reasonably reliable large, white-flowered clematis suitable for mid- to late-summer flowering. 3m (10ft) with a similar spread.

Clematis tangutica, C. orientalis

Deciduous rambler. These clematis flower from late summer to early winter, with yellow bell-shaped blooms. The latter is commonly called the orange-peel clematis, which is a good description for the flowers, otherwise they are similar plants with yellow or orange flowers on a framework which reaches 3m (10ft) with a similar spread. Works well when grown through a deciduous tree.

Clematis viticella

Deciduous rambler. Colours from white through pink, red and purple, depending upon the variety, and a flowering season in late summer. Its growth habit and the fact that it should be pruned in March makes it the perfect companion for climbing roses. Try *C. v.* 'Abundance' with *Rosa* 'New Dawn'. 3m (10ft) with a similar spread.

✿ *Clematis* **'Abundance'** and *Rosa* **'New Dawn'**.

Euonymus fortunei

Self-clinging evergreen shrub. Usually grown as a free-standing shrub, this plant will climb a wall using rootlets, in a similar way to ivy. The best climbers are 'Silver Queen' and 'Emerald 'n' Gold', but they all have the ability. 1.5m (5ft) by 1.2m (4ft).

Ficus carica (Fig)

Deciduous shrub. The large palmate leaves make this one of the best architectural plants available. It can be grown as a free-standing shrub, but needs a warm wall if the fruit is to ripen successfully. 'Brown Turkey' is the best variety. For details of growing as a fruiting plant see page 110. 4m (13ft) with a similar spread.

Fremontodendron californicum (Fremontia)

Evergreen wall shrub. This tall, narrow growing shrub has one of the longest flowering seasons of all. Its large yellow saucer-shaped flowers appear in May and are still being produced in the autumn. Grow it alongside climbing ceanothus. The leaf and stems are covered in tiny hairs, which can irritate if they make contact with skin, or even worse the eye, so keep it away from a main doorway. It can be pruned back quite hard, if necessary. 5m (16ft) by 1.8m (6ft).

Garrya elliptica 'James Roof' (Silk tassel bush)

Evergreen wall shrub. The long silver catkins of this shrub are a welcome diversion in the heart of the winter. It is a large shrub that is happier on a cool wall, although it will grow in sun. 3m (10ft) with a similar spread.

Hederas (Ivies)

Few evergreen climbers are totally hardy in the British Isles, elevating the tough and reliable ivy into a place of its own. This has led to them being planted widely, therefore developing an unjust reputation for being boring, and they are often planted only as a last resort. They climb using tiny rootlets which cling to the wall, avoiding the need for any support but frightening people into thinking that they will damage brickwork. This fear is generally unfounded – damage is only done to brickwork which already has problems, although removing ivy can leave rather unfortunate scars which are difficult to clean away.

Wild ivy will often grow through trees. I personally don't like the look of it however many people believe that it is a way of extending the season of interest for a deciduous tree. It cannot do much harm, unless the ivy covers the whole tree and blots out the light.

There are a vast number of different ivies now available, and some nurseries specialize in them. This diversity can make it difficult to find a particular variety, but the following four are not difficult to find and should cover all requirements.

Hedera canariensis 'Gloire de Marengo'.

Evergreen rambler. The Canary island ivies have large oval-shaped leaves and this one also has white variegation. It is rather reluctant to climb and needs some encouragement, especially when young. 3m (10ft) by 3m.

Hedera helix 'Cristata'

Evergreen rambler. Plain green with an unusual crinkled edge to the leaf, this tough climber is good in informal planting schemes. 3m (10ft) with a similar spread.

Hedera helix 'Glacier'

Evergreen rambler. Another small-leafed ivy. This one has a white variegation in the leaf and looks good against red brick. 3m (10ft) with a similar spread.

Hedera helix 'Gold Heart'

Evergreen rambler. Quite similar to 'Glacier', but the leaves are slightly larger and each has a yellow centre. 3m (10ft) with a similar spread.

Humulus lupulus 'Aureus' (Golden hop)

Deciduous rambler. This plant is more like a climbing herbaceous perennial than a traditional climber, as it regrows from the ground every year. It is very fast, and robust enough to cover a small shed in a single season. The soft yellow foliage makes a fine contrast for many darker colours in the garden. 5m (16ft) with a similar spread.

Hydrangea petiolaris (Climbing hydrangea)

Deciduous rambler. This self-clinging climber is the first choice for a north-facing wall or fence, where it clings using tiny rootlets, in a similar way to ivy. It is notorious, when young, for being slow to start growing; during this time it is developing its root system and it can take up to four years before it starts to climb. Once it starts to climb it does so rapidly. The flowers are like those of a white lacecap hydrangea. 6m (20ft) with a similar spread.

Itea ilicifolia (Sweetspire)

Evergreen lax shrub. I love this plant. Its flowers have the appearance of long catkins, are sweetly scented and appear in August, perhaps the best time to appreciate this plant's characteristics. It is very slow-growing, however, and may take several years to reach any significant height. Needs a sheltered wall. 1.5m (5ft) by 1.2m (4ft).

❀ ***Humulus lupulus* 'Aureus' – the golden hop.**

Jasminum nudiflorum (Winter jasmine)

Deciduous wall shrub. This plant is so widely planted that many people think of it when the term jasmine is used. It can be grown as a free-standing rambling shrub, looking especially attractive on a bank. Its yellow flowers appear in profusion right through the winter, so it must be planted where its flowers can be appreciated. When grown against a wall it must be kept tied in and under control or it may become a problem. 3m (10ft) with a similar spread.

Jasminum officinale (Jasmine)

Deciduous rambler. The heady scent of jasmine on a summer's evening should be enjoyed by everyone, so it is worth making the effort to include this plant in every garden. It will grow in sun or shade, but sometimes refuses to flower in either aspect – it just seems to take a dislike to some gardens! 6m (20ft) by 6m.

☑ ✴ ✴ ✴ ✌ ◀ ▨

Jasminum × stephanense (Jasmine)

Deciduous rambler. This plant is similar to *J. officinale*, but with pink flowers held on a less vigorous plant. 3m (10ft) by 3m.

◎ ✴ ✴ ✴ ✌ ◀ ▨

Honeysuckles

These are among the most popular climbing plants and almost every garden has at least one. The best scented form is *Lonicera periclymenum*, but as with all the deciduous varieties it is extremely untidy, soon becoming top-heavy and dead at the base. Either hide it, where you can smell it but not see it, or plant a better-behaved evergreen version. Note: plants like *Lonicera pileata*, *L. nitida* or *L. fragrantissimum*, although related to honeysuckle, are free-standing shrubs, and not for training against a wall.

Lonicera japonica henryii (Evergreen honeysuckle)

Evergreen rambler. This honeysuckle has an open growth and is easier to train across a fence or trellis than other honeysuckles. Purple/red/yellow clusters of flowers. 5m (16ft) by 5m.

◎ ✴ ✴ ✴ ✌ ◀

Lonicera periclymenum (Honeysuckle)

Deciduous rambler. For sweet scents, nothing beats this plant, but its untidiness means that it needs to be carefully placed. 3m (10ft)with a similar spread.

☑ ✴ ✴ ✴ ✌ ◀ ▨

Magnolia grandiflora (Evergreen magnolia)

Evergreen shrub. This flowering shrub is truly spectacular when in flower,with magnificent white scented water-lily-like blooms in late summer and early autumn. The plant is very upright-growing and benefits from a wall to offer it support, but it needs plenty of space. It can also be grown as a free-standing shrub/tree in the warmer counties. 2m (6ft 6in) by 1.5m (5ft).

◎ ✴ ✴ ✴ ✌ ◀

Parthenocissus henryana (Chinese Virginia creeper)

Deciduous climber. This self-clinging plant (it climbs by sucker pads rather than rootlets like ivy) is the Virginia creeper for a north wall. The leaves have a white stripe down the centre and turn to a brilliant red in the autumn. 5m (16ft)with a similar spread.

◎ ✴ ✴ ✴ ✌ ◀ ▨

Parthenocissus tricuspidata 'Veitchii' (Boston ivy)

Deciduous climber. When ordinary Virginia creeper, *P. quinquefolia*, is planted it is often this plant, Boston ivy, which everyone expects. Virginia creeper hates to climb, preferring to scurry across the ground, and needs some encouragement, whereas Boston Ivy revels in covering a wall or trying to turning a house into a hedge. The last phrase represents a warning: this plant, and *P. henryana* above, are robust and rampant so do not plant them unless you are prepared to accept their ways.
6m (20ft)with a similar spread.

◎ ✴ ✴ ✴ ✌ ◀ ▨

Passiflora caerulea (Passion flower)

Evergreen rambler. Given perfect conditions – a hot sheltered wall – this plant can grow very large, outgrowing its allocated space and becoming a small nuisance. Away from this shelter it is less vigorous and its hardiness suspect in the cooler counties. The flowers are exotic, fragrant and extremely unusual. 5m (16ft) with a similar spread.

☑ ✴ ✴ ✌ ◀

Pyracantha 'Mojave' (Firethorn)

Evergreen shrub. As a free-standing plant, a pyracantha will reach 3m (10ft) in both height and spread. This needs to be borne in mind when one is planted as a climber; it needs a lot of training or it will become uncontrollable and the thorns can do a lot of damage. 'Mojave' has white flowers in spring and orange berries in late summer. Any pyracantha will do, but this one has the benefit of being easy to obtain.

☑ ✴ ✴ ✴ ✌ ◀ ▨

Climbing Roses

Most gardens have at least one climbing rose, but few are a great success. The parentage of roses is so diverse that a climber may require a warm or a cool wall and this is often the reason that climbing roses are unsuccessful. Often, simply moving the plant to a different aspect can solve the problem.

plant lists

Soil
PH Must have an acid soil
Can cope with a light, dry sandy soil
C Grow well in clay soil
Will grow in any soil, but not damp
Will grow in damp or boggy conditions

Habit
G Good groundcover –the plant smothers the soil, stopping seeds from germinating.
M Some groundcover – the soil is covered but not enough to stop germination.
P Poor groundcover – there is a lot of bare soil around the plant.

Planting times
(these represent the optimum time of the year to plant – for more details see page 12)
◧ Spring
◨ Autumn
▦ Summer

The following roses cover most colours and aspects; I have also included one or two curiosities:

Rosa 'Danse du Feu'.

Red is always a difficult colour for rose breeders, and plants with this colour flower rarely come up to the quality of other roses. This one is not perfect, often suffering from mildew and blackspot, but it is red, and flowers all summer with dark green foliage. 2.4m (8ft) with a similar spread.

Rosa 'Golden Showers'

Covered with yellow blooms all summer long, perhaps the most floriferous of all roses. Plant close to *Cytisus battandieri*. 3m (10ft) with a similar spread.

Rosa 'Madame Alfred Carrière'

Picture a traditional cottage door surrounded by a rambling rose and you will have pictured this plant. It has white scented flowers, which appear continuously and is happy in any aspect, including north-facing. It is vigorous enough to cover a pergola or even to climb through a tree. 4m (13ft) by 3m (10ft).

Rosa 'Mermaid'

Large, creamy white, saucer-shaped flowers give this plant a place of its own among roses. The display is spectacular in late June and early July, but is not continuous, although there are occasional flowers produced into the autumn. 3m (10ft) with a similar spread.

Rosa 'Morning Jewel'

Many climbers, not just roses, suffer from being top-heavy when growing on fences or walls – the flowers appear on the top with nothing lower down. This plant is different – the bright pink flowers are held on the plant right down to the ground. One magnificent display in late June and early July is followed by occasional flowers into the autumn. 2.4m (8ft) with a similar spread.

Rosa 'New Dawn'

Good disease-resistance and a long flowering season make this one of the best pink scented climbers. It is a rambler and is perfect over a pergola or arbour. Grow it with *Clematis viticella*

'Abundance'. *R.* 'Penny Lane', Rose of the Year in 1998, is another pink climber which could prove to be even better. 4m (13ft) by 3m (10ft).

Rosa 'Nice Day'

This is a miniature climber, perfect for a small space, and will even grow in a container. The flowers are pink and appear continuously. 1.8m (6ft) by 1.2m (4ft).

Rosa 'Zéphirine Drouhin'

This plant stands out because it is one of the few thornless roses, making it the essential choice for certain applications. The flowers are cerise pink and very fragrant, appearing continuously. 3m (10ft) with a similar spread.

Solanum jasminoides 'Album' (Jasmine nightshade)

Deciduous rambler. I find this a more refined climber than the blue flowered climbing potato, *S. crispum* 'Glasnevin's Variety', which is difficult to control in a small garden. Both have a very long flowering season. 'Album' needs some shelter, preferably on a south-facing wall. It is quite fast-growing and covers a lot of ground in a single season, but is easily controlled. The flowers are white and very fragrant. 3m (10ft) with a similar spread.

Trachelospermum jasminoides (Star jasmine)

Evergreen rambler. We are pitifully short of evergreen climbers which are hardy enough in our climate. This one is the best. As the name suggests, it is an evergreen jasmine, with sweetly scented white flowers in midsummer. It must have a protected wall, facing south or west, to be at its best. Not difficult to find, but may not appear in the garden centre until May or June. 2.4m (8ft) by 2m (6ft 6in).

Tropaeolum speciosum (Flame creeper)

Deciduous rambler. Nothing is more eye-catching than the flame creeper growing through a dark green conifer hedge. It has been included because it is one of the gems of the garden, but is difficult to establish (two out of three plants will die). 1.8m (6ft) by 90cm (9ft).

Vitis coignetiae (Crimson glory vine)

Deciduous rambler. This large-leafed vine makes a bold,

Key to codes

Availability
☑ **Easily obtainable. Should be available anywhere.**
◎ **May require some searching or could be seasonal, but should not be too difficult to find.**
⬆ **Best to order from a specialist nursery.**

Conditions **Sun or shade**
❋ **Shade**
❋ **Part shade**
❋ **Full sun**

impressive display, but it requires careful placing as it is a large plant and can dominate a garden. The foliage turns crimson and scarlet in the autumn before the leaves drop. 6m (20ft) with a similar spread.

☑ ❋ ❋ ❋ ▨ ▤ ▨

Vitis vinifera 'Brant' (Ornamental Grape Vine)
Deciduous rambler. The grape vine is one of the best plants for either sun or shade. This variety, although it does develop grapes, is grown mainly for its excellent foliage, which turns a startling mixture of copper, orange and red in the autumn. Excellent for creating the right atmosphere over a pergola, it complements all forms of wooden structures, even garden seats. 6m (20ft) by 6m.

◎ ❋ ❋ ❋ ▨ ▤ ▨

Vitis vinifera 'Purpurea' (Teinturier grape)
Deciduous rambler. Another vine, but this one has wine-coloured leaves. 4m (13ft) with a similar spread.

◎ ❋ ❋ ▨ ▤ ▨

Wisteria sinensis
Deciduous rambler. Mellow red brick on south- or west-facing façades are crying out for the hanging lilac flowers of this stately plant. It is fast growing, but could take up to fifteen years before it produces its first flower. To avoid this wait, buy a plant that has been grafted using material from a plant already flowering. 10m (33ft) with a similar spread.

☑ ❋ ❋ ▨ ▤ ▨

Plants with a health warning

Many plants are planted in our gardens without any thought, or knowledge, of how they will behave over the following years. Some plants turn wild and run amok, while others simply die without warning. This section consists of plants which, for one reason or another, can become a problem. It is not a comprehensive list, but it does cover many of the more popular plants and represents my experiences, either personally or by observing other people's gardens.

The biggest problem group are plants with invasive tendencies which, once planted, get such a tight grip on their surroundings that they become a weed in their own right – usually herbaceous perennials, through there are one or two examples among the shrubs. With herbaceous plants, look at the top of the soil in the pot: if the plant is going to be invasive then new shoots will be growing around the edge of the pot, showing that the root system is waiting for the opportunity to escape into your garden. If the plant has formed a clump in the centre of the pot you should be safe.

Having said this, colonizing plants do have their uses. They will often grow in harsh conditions where most other plants cannot cope and, the conditions often mean that their invasive tendency is checked. Plants like *Euphorbia amygdaroides robbiae* and *Anemone x hybrida* (Japanese anemone) can be a nuisance in perfect conditions but are a boon in dry shade. Because of this, some plants appear both here and in the recommended plants list.

Water garden plants nearly all have invasive tendencies and should always be grown in baskets specially designed to sit just above or below the water's surface. If allowed to grow 'loose' they will quickly clog up a small to medium-sized pond to the exclusion of everything else.

Plants in these lists should not necessarily be avoided (except those on page 153), but you should be aware of the problems involved with them.

Plants with a gentle warning
The following is a list of plants, frequently planted in the wrong place, wrong conditions or require more care than expected.

Acanthus mollis, A. spinosa (Bear's breeches)
In clay soil this plant can be well-behaved – once established the clump will slowly, inexorably spread outwards, but nevertheless it is not a great problem. In a light soil, in perfect conditions, it can be a rogue. The deep roots make it extremely difficult to remove, so care must be taken in getting its location right first time.

Alstromerias (Peruvian lily)
The most curious thing about this plant is that it comes from Chile, not Peru. But the alliteration in the name 'Chile lily' was too much for those who discovered it, so they called it the Peruvian lily. The reason for the warning is that the species is very invasive. There are, however, some new strains, many of which are dwarf, which the growers claim to be well-behaved.

Anemone x hybrida (Japanese anemone)
This plant behaves in a similar way to acanthus, in that it can be robust and invasive in certain conditions and therefore requires careful placing. It will, however, grow and flower in very dry shade.

Astilbes (False goat's beard)
These plants must have damp soil. Too often they are planted in ordinary soil, where they survive for a short time before gradually fading away.

Soil
- **PH** Must have an acid soil
- Can cope with a light, dry sandy soil
- **C** Grow well in clay soil
- Will grow in any soil, but not damp
- Will grow in damp or boggy conditions

Habit
- **G** Good groundcover –the plant smothers the soil, stopping seeds from germinating.
- **M** Some groundcover – the soil is covered but not enough to stop germination.
- **P** Poor groundcover – there is a lot of bare soil around the plant.

Planting times
(these represent the optimum time of the year to plant – for more details see page 12)
- Spring
- Autumn
- Summer

Buddleia alternifolia (Fountain buddleia)
Many people do not realise it can grow to the size of a small tree. As with other buddleias, it grows very quickly and can reach a substantial size in a season. It also flowers much earlier. Make sure that it has enough space - 3m (9ft) by 2.5m (8ft 3in).

Cerastium tomentosum (Snow-in-Summer)
Evergreen grey foliage covered in white flowers in the height of summer ought to make this plant one of the prizes of the garden. It can, however, be a nuisance and never really looks tidy.

Clematis (large-leafed)
Many of the large flowered hybrids are difficult and can be a disappointment in the garden. Better to choose hybrids with medium-sized flowers such as 'Hagley Hybrid' or 'Ville de Lyon'.

Clematis montana
This clematis has an outstanding display of flowers in May, but is a large and vigorous plant which is often planted where there is not sufficient space.

Conifers
There are many problems associated with conifers, most connected to their size, but there is also a problem in planting them in a mixed scheme. With the notable exception of yew, most conifers do not have any dormant buds in their trunk and branches so if any external foliage dies it will not grow back.

Cortaderia selloana (Pampas grass)
In the right conditions, in a large garden, this plant is magnificent. Far too often, though, it is planted in small gardens where it can be a real problem. Each leaf is like a long thin razor blade and can do a lot of damage, unless gloves are worn; it needs at least a 2m diameter circle in which to grow, which it does not often get. *Stipa gigantea* is a grass which is similar in shape and style, but which requires much less space.

Cupressocyparis leylandii (Leyland cypress)
This is the fastest-growing conifer and for that reason is planted on a massive scale as screening hedging. It can make a good, solid, pleasant-looking screen, but requires careful trimming and attention which, sadly, it rarely gets. Problems: it grows too fast; it takes moisture out of the ground which has been cited as causing damage to houses; it upsets neighbours by blotting out their light; unless nurtured early enough and continuously maintained it will open up at the base and look very untidy.

Cytisus (Broom)
Bright and colourful flowers in the spring have made these plants very popular. The colour is fleeting and the plant itself contributes little to the garden when not in flower. It does not respond to pruning and has no ground covering properties.

Forsythia
This yellow-flowered shrub should be a welcome sign of spring, but is so common that its impact is lost. In a small garden it doesn't earn its keep: a few weeks of flower in the spring is all the plant can offer. The rest of the year it contributes little to the garden.

Ericas (Heathers)
There is a myth that these plants are low-maintenance ground-cover gems. Their pink, white and mauve flowers make a fine display, especially on a heather moor, but they become straggly and untidy about two years after planting and are best replaced. Most people have visions of a rolling garden covered with heathers and conifers; a vision conjured up in a number of famous places. What is not usually known is that the heathers in these gardens are replaced every other year to maintain the effect. Also, heathers are happiest in acid soil, the winter-flowering varieties being the only ones which will tolerate alkalinity.

Eucalyptus gunnii
In the wild, this evergreen tree grows to around 30 m (100ft) in height, most of which consists of a tall single white-barked trunk. As a small plant, the foliage is a dusty blue which always looks attractive in the garden centre. Once planted, however, it is very fast-growing and quickly develops its tall white trunk, its foliage reverting to a dull grey. If you want to plant one, cut it down to 30cm from the ground every spring and it will become a small shrub, retaining the attractive blue foliage of the young plant.

Euphorbia amygdaloides robbiae (Spurge)
The acid-green flowers of this plant make it a fine companion for most flower colours. The problem is that, in ideal conditions, it can be invasive and will swamp its neighbours. Best reserved for those difficult shady spots.

Fallopia baldschnanica (Polygonum baldschuanicum) (Russian vine, mile-a-minute vine)
Purported to be the fastest-growing climber, a fact that attracts many people when they want to cover something quickly. The problem is that it doesn't stop growing and becomes a large, untidy monster. If you want to cover an eyesore, try *Humulus lupulus* 'Aureus' – the golden hop.

Key to codes

Availability
☑ **Easily obtainable. Should be available anywhere.**
🔍 **May require some searching or could be seasonal, but should not be too difficult to find.**
🏠 **Best to order from a specialist nursery.**

Conditions **Sun or shade**
✸ **Shade**
✸ **Part shade**
✸ **Full sun**

Juniperus × media 'Pfitzeriana'

Often sold in garden centres dwarf and low-growing conifer. Even the Royal Horticultural Society encyclopaedia lists it as a 'dwarf'. It is nothing of the sort. It will grow to at least 3m (10ft) in height with a spread of 5m (15ft) plus. Unless you have a very large garden and enough space, avoid this plant like the plague. If you want a genuinely dwarf low-growing, well-behaved conifer, try *Juniperus communis* 'Green Carpet' or one of the *J. squamata* hybrids.

Lupinus polyphyllus (Herbaceous lupins)

Not to be confused with *L. arboreus*, the tree lupin. These popular garden plants really need a well-drained acid soil, on which they will thrive for many years. On alkaline soil they are very short-lived and are best treated as biennial – replaced after the second year; left until the third year they will be very poor plants and will eventually fade away.

Melianthus major (Honey bush)

The bold foliage of this plant is such a striking addition to a design that it seems churlish to warn of its shortcomings. The problem is that it is very invasive and will pop up all over a flower bed; this is bad enough in a small plant, but with such large foliage this plant is a real nuisance.

Papaver hybrids (Poppies)

The large red-flowered oriental poppies are a delight when in flower; the problem is that after flowering the whole plant collapses, leaving an unfortunate gap in the border. Gertrude Jekyll, the great plantswoman from the beginning of this century, always planted gypsophila behind her poppies so that it could grow over the space left by the poppies after they had flowered.

Parthenocissus quinquefolia (Virginia creeper)

Most people plant this with visions of a self-clinging climbing plant that will quickly cover a large wall or structure with foliage which turns a rich red in autumn. The plant people have in mind is actually Boston ivy, *Parthenocissus tricuspidata* 'Veitchii' – whereas true Virginia creeper would rather trail and scurry across the ground, avoiding the structure it is intended to cover.

Solanum crispum 'Glasnevin's Variety' (Climbing potato)

A lovely plant, but one which needs a lot of space, a lot of pruning and a lot of tying in to keep it under control.

Syringa (Lilac)

This is a warning against planting the larger lilacs in a small garden. They have a short flowering season and a mat-forming root system that virtually excludes any underplanting. There are some smaller varieties however: *S. meyeri* 'Palabin' (the Korean lilac) or *S. microphylla* 'Superba'.

Plants that I no longer include in my gardens

Over the years the list of plants I include in my planting plans has evolved, with plants being continually added and deleted. The reasons for dropping them are varied, but valid for anyone who is creating a garden.

Acer griseum (Paper bark maple)

This has to be one of the loveliest of garden trees. So why is it here? The reason is that it is so slow-growing that it is difficult to find a plant larger than 90cm (3ft) in height and even at that size it will cost a small fortune. Although inferior, *Prunus serrula*, the paperbark cherry, is a viable alternative.

Geranium 'Johnson's Blue'

It is difficult to determine the size each plant will grow to. In some conditions it would swamp its neighbours, in others it would develop very poorly. It is not a long-flowering plant and I now prefer to select a longer-flowering hardy geraniums.

Hemerocallis 'Pink Damask'

This is a lovely plant with a genuinely pink flower, unusual for something developed from a predominantly yellow- or orange-flowered species. And this is the problem. Whenever I have used it in a planting scheme, the nursery has sent it in a bewildering range of yellows, oranges or browns – but rarely pink! If you are going to buy this plant, either look for it in flower or buy it from a specialist nursery.

Iris tectorum 'Variegata'

This plant was originally sent to me by a nurseryman as a viable alternative to *Iris foetidissima* 'Variegata', mainly because it is also evergreen. It is very invasive and does not stay where it has been planted. It is frequently labelled up wrongly in the garden centre, so check any variegated irises and if they are growing around the edge of the container and appear to be trying to escape, then leave them alone and look elsewhere.

Potentilla fruticosa 'Manchu'

The true plant flowers all summer, with dainty white rose-like flowers on a ground-hugging mat of grey foliage. Unfortunately, the large *P.* 'Abbotswood White' is often sold with this label on it; so much so that it has become impractical to select the plant. If the plant does not have grey foliage hugging the surface of the soil and perhaps even the side of the container, then it is not 'Manchu'.

Stachys byzantina 'Silver Carpet' (Lamb's ears)

Gertrude Jekyll always removed the flowers from lamb's ears as they are ugly and cause the plant to lose its shape. Eventually a non-flowering variety was bred called 'Silver Carpet'. When this plant became popular nobody wanted the ordinary *S. byzantina* and unscrupulous nurserymen relabelled them as 'Silver Carpet'. It is now almost impossible to find the true 'Silver Carpet' which is a shame, as it is one of the best front-of-border plants available, especially alongside a path or patio. Only plant this if it has been obtained as a cutting from a known non-flowering plant, or ordered from a specialist nurseryman who can guarantee it.

Plants to avoid at all costs

Some plants are such a nuisance, or a danger, that they should never be planted in the private garden.

Aconitum napellus (Monkshood)

The whole plant is very poisonous. There are a lot of myths about plants being poisonous, much of which is unfounded because the volume of plant material which must be consumed is extremely high. This plant is different. Small doses can lead to unpleasant side-effects, and tales of dogs dying from playing with the roots are not exaggerated. Lupins, delphiniums, acanthus and perovskias will achieve the same effect but with less danger.

Buddleia globosa

This is a very large plant, requiring a lot of room for which it does not pay well. The flowers only last for a short time and are the worst shade of orange and a very unnatural pom-pom shape whilst there is little of interest about the rest of the plant.

Carex pendula (Pendulous sedge)

This native grass often seeds itself into our gardens, where it is at first welcomed until its invasive coarseness is appreciated.

Equisetum (Horsetail)

Most gardeners are introduced to these plants when the small Christmas-tree type growth of field horsetail appears in their garden, where it is the worst of all pernicious weeds. Ornamental varieties, used mainly around the edge of lakes and in shallow ponds. Not only will it clog up the water course, but it will rapidly spread into the surrounding borders. Weedkiller will have only a very limited effect upon it and it is difficult to eradicate by hand.

Hyacinthoides non-scripta (Bluebell)

There is nothing like walking through a bluebell wood in April, but had you noticed that there are very few other low plants growing alongside it? This plant does not stand for any competition and simply smothers any opposition. Occasionally it will seed itself into a private garden, and will then proceed to multiply itself and kill off any other plants in the garden. Remove it should it appear and do not plant it.

Lamium (Dead nettle)

Another invasive plant which most people plant as groundcover to reduce maintenance, only to find themselves introducing a pernicious weed.

Phalaris arundinacea var. picta (Gardeners' garters)

Grasses and bamboos have an undeserved reputation for being invasive, and this plant must take most of the blame for these misunderstandings. Its attractively variegated foliage disguises the fact that it spreads like wildfire. If you want a variegated grass try one of the sedges – *Carex oshimensis* 'Evergold' or *C. morrowii* 'Fishers Form' which has a more creamy stripe to the leaf. For a taller plant try *Miscanthus sinensis* 'Zebrinus'.

Physalis (Chinese lanterns)

Another highly invasive plant which is difficult to deal with once it becomes established.

Sasu veitchii (Bamboo)

Most grasses and bamboos are well-behaved but this one is a great spreader, sending its root system off in different directions. The best place to plant it is on an island in a pond or lake.

Symphoricarpus (Snowberry)

I can see no reason for planting this plant in any private garden. It forms a dense thicket that is very difficult to eradicate once established.

Vinca major, Vinca major 'Variegata' (Greater Periwinkle)

This pernicious weed has large blue flowers that appear in April. Once planted in the garden it often reverts, losing its attractive variegated leaves, and its invasive roots begin to spread out like tentacles! It has tough, weedkiller-resistant foliage – a real survivor and difficult to eradicate.

✿ **Warm colours and good design combine here to create a welcoming garden.**

Glossary

Acid vs. Alkaline. Some plants, generally known as ericaceous, must have an acid soil in which to grow otherwise they could die, whereas plants which prefer an alkaline soil will tolerate an acid one. An acid soil has a pH less than 7.0 and alkaline of more; 7.0 being neutral.

Algae. A simple plant which will quickly colonize open water exposed to too much light. Can be in the form of a thick thread-like mass, just a green slimy layer or a colouring in the water.

Alpine planting mixture. Two parts potting compost, one part sharp sand and a generous sprinkling of bonemeal.

Aerobic. Full of oxygen.

Anaerobic. Lacking in oxygen.

Annual. A plant which naturally dies after less than one year of independent life, survival of the race depending entirely on the production of seed.

Aphid. A sap-sucking insect commonly called greenfly or blackfly.

Ball-rooted. A way of transporting open ground trees and shrubs: the rootball and surrounding soil is dug up and wrapped in hessian or a similar material.

Bamboo. A term referring to a group of grass-like shrubs. *Arundinaria, Bambusa, Fargesia, Phyllostachys, Pleioblastus* and *Sasa* are all commonly grown bamboos.

Bare-rooted. Usually refers to open-ground trees and shrubs that have been dug up during the winter months for sale. A common way of selling roses and specimen trees.

Bed. An area of open soil planted with ornamental garden plants.

Biennial. A plant which devotes its first year of life to the development of large reserves of nutritive materials and then flowers and dies in the second.

Blackfly. Another name for a variety of aphid.

Blanket weed. An algae which forms a mat of emerald-green filaments in open water. Best removed by twisting around a rough twig. Difficult to eradicate.

Border. Usually refers to a bed around the edge of the garden, or a feature within it, but sometimes also used as a general term for a flower bed.

Brindle. Refers to the colour of bricks, or pavers, where the predominant colour is red, but this is impregnated with other colours, usually blacks and browns.

Coir. The waste material from coconut production. Usually seen in a composted form and sold as a substitute for peat or forest bark. Claims that it is the revolutionary new saviour of the environment are suspect; damage caused to the natural environment from which it is extracted is not reported.

Curiously, this discovery was in frequent use by the Victorians.

Cordon. Used to describe a trained fruit tree which has one or more stems.

Deadheading. The removal of dead flower heads, usually to promote the production of more flowers.

Deciduous. A term used to describe a plant which loses its leaves every autumn and grows fresh ones in the spring.

Dibber. A tool used for planting. Usually a piece of round wood, about 4cm (1.5in) in diameter and tapered at one end.

Dormant. Used by gardeners to describe deciduous plants which have ceased active growth for the year.

Dormant bud. A shoot on a stem which is waiting to grow.

Ericaceous. Used to describe plants which need an acid soil.

Evergreen. A term referring to plants which retain their foliage through the whole year. Despite the inference, evergreen plants do jettison old leaves, sometimes continuously, like holly, or seasonally, like bergenias which dispose of old leaves after flowering.

Exposed aggregate. Concrete, where the top surface of cement has been washed away to expose the aggregate. If done correctly, it can look like rough gravel, but benefits from being a more solid surface.

Fastigiate. Upright, columnar. Used to describe the habit of a plant.

Frog. Apart from being a useful carnivorous amphibian, this is a term use to describe an indentation in a brick which allows more cement to be used between bricks.

Garden centre. More akin to a gardeners' supermarket. They rarely grow their own, but buy their stock in. Can be expensive, but plants are usually guaranteed for up to two years which can be useful.

Germinate. The first beginnings of independent growth. Usually refers to the first signs of life in a seed.

Grafting. A method of joining two woody plants together.

Greenfly. Another name for a variety of aphid.

Glyphosate. A systemic weed-killing chemical.

Hardworks. A term used to describe garden structures: paths, walls, etc.

Header pool. The highest pool in a waterfall or rill water feature.

Heeling in. A term used to describe how bare-rooted plants are loosely planted for use at a later date in the garden.

Hoggin. A material consisting of clay, sand and gravel, used for constructing paths. Often a waste material from gravel pits.

Hybrid. The offspring of two markedly different parents. The whole area of hybridization is complex, but it is worth knowing that many hybrids are either sterile or have poor fertility.

Inorganic. A term usually used to describe anything in the garden which is dead or has never been alive.

In the green. Generally used to describe the planting of bulbs when they are actively growing. Snowdrops and winter aconites are best planted this way.

John Innes. A term referring to soil-based compost. Developed by the John Innes Institute.

MOT. A term used by contractors to refer to loose chippings and dust, usually granite, which is generally used as hardcore.

Mulch. Material, either organic or inorganic, laid on the surface of the soil around plants to conserve moisture and help keep weeds under control.

Mulching mat. Man-made loosely woven material used to cover the ground. The open weave allows water through but keeps weeds and their seeds in the dark.

Nursery. A place which grows its own plants from seed or cuttings. Often specializing in particular types or varieties of plant.

Open ground. A term used to refer to nursery plants which are grown in the open ground rather than in containers.

Organic. Refers to anything in the garden which is, or has been, alive.

pH. Used to determine the level of acidity in either water or soil. pH 7.0 is neutral, anything higher than 7.0 is alkaline, lower is acid.

Pollinator. A term usually used in fruit-growing where cross-pollination is required for successful germination; the pollinator being the plant which supplies the pollen. Apples and most pears need a pollinator.

Pot on. A term used to describe how plants are transferred into larger pots as they grow.

Pressure-treated. Refers to soft wood which has been treated with a preservative to extend its life. Pressure refers to the process of forcing the chemical into the centre of the wood. To be properly pressure-treated, wood has to go through a process which includes kiln drying before the chemical is applied. This has resulted in a lot of inferior pressure-treated wood. The only way to determine if the wood is truly pressure-treated is to ask for a guarantee. It should be guaranteed for at least twenty-five years.

Propagation. Refers to a variety of methods used to generate new plants.

Reversion. Plants with variegated foliage are in fact a mistake as far as nature is concerned, and many will produce branches with plain green foliage. This plain green foliage is where the plant is attempting to revert to its original form. Any reverted foliage should be removed completely or the plant will completely return to its original colour.

Rhizomes. An underground shoot which is roughly horizontal (most are subterranean, but some, like those of the iris, lie on the surface). The underground root system of bindweed, ground elder, couch grass and field horsetail described on page 78 is in fact a system of rhizomes.

Rootballed. A method of transporting bare-rooted trees and shrubs. The plant is dug up, usually with a soil ball attached, and encased in sacking for transportation.

Sequestered iron. Basically, iron dissolved in water. Used to water acid loving plants growing in neutral or slightly alkaline soil.

Skirt. A term referring to the base of a shrub which grows downwards smothering the soil.

Specimen. A plant which has been grown in a container, or in open ground, for a number of years, and is sold as a much larger plant than is normally available.

Standard rose. A rose trained on a single stem. A rose tree.

Standards. Plants, usually shrubs, trained as trees.

Subsoil. The poor soil below the topsoil, often anaerobic and lacking in organic material and therefore a poor growing medium.

Systemic. A term referring to weedkillers or insecticides which work by invading the system of a plant.

Tap-root. The main vertical root of a plant.

Top-dressing. A term used to describe any plant food or soil improver applied to the top of the soil, but not incorporated.

Top grafting. A method of creating a larger tree without waiting for it to grow. A choice plant is attached to the top of a faster-growing plant's trunk. Sometimes top-grafting is necessary, as with the Kilmarnock willow, which does not create a trunk of its own, but generally trees created in this way are best avoided as they often deteriorate with age.

Top growth. That part of the plant above the ground.

Top pruning. Taking out the leaders to encourage a bushier growth further down.

Topsoil. Garden soil for planting.

Tufa. A limestone deposit, often thought of as rock. Very soft and used as a container for tiny alpines, which are planted directly into holes carved in it.

Type 1. Another term for MOT.

Type 2. A finer grade MOT.

Water table. Used to describe the level of any natural subterranean water. In extreme cases a high water table will result in water filling a recently dug hole.

Useful addresses

National Council for the
Conservation of Plants and
Gardens (NCCPG)
Stable Courtyard
RHS Garden
Wisley
Woking
Surrey
GU23 6QP

Henry Doubleday Research
Association (Soil Association)
Ryton Organic Gardens
Ryton on Dunsmore
Coventry
Warwickshire
CV8 3LG

Arboricultural Association
Ampfield House
Ampfield
Romsey
Hants
SO51 9PA

Royal National Rose Society
The Gardens of the Rose
Chiswell Green
St Albans
Herts
AL2 3NR

Alpine Garden Society
AGS Centre
Pershore College of Horticulture
Avonbank
Pershore
Worcs
WR10 3JP

British Association of Landscape
Industries (BALI)
Landscape House
9 Henry St
Keighley
W. Yorkshire
BD21 3DR

Royal Horticultural Society (RHS)
80 Vincent Square
London
SW1P 2PE

Hardy Plant Society
Little Orchard
Great Comberton
Pershore
Worcs
WR10 3DP

Bibliography

The Royal Horticultural Society Plant Finder, Moorland Publishing, published annually.
Brian Davis and Brian Knapp, *Know Your Common Plant Names,* MDA Publications, 1992.
Graham A. Pavey, *Start to Plant Alpine and Rock Gardens,* Apple Press, 1996.
Graham Stuart Thomas, *Perennial Garden Plants,* Dent, 1976.
Nigel J. Taylor, *Ornamental Grasses, Bamboos, Rushes and Sedges,* Ward Lock, 1992.

Index

creative gardening for busy people